Harcourt
Health
and
Fitness

 **Harcourt**
SCHOOL PUBLISHERS

Orlando • Austin • New York • San Diego • Toronto • London

Visit *The Learning Site!*
www.harcourtschool.com

CONSULTING AUTHORS

Lisa Bunting, M.Ed.
Physical Education Teacher
Katy Independent School District
Houston, Texas

Thomas M. Fleming, Ph.D.
Health and Physical Education
    Consultant
Lenoir City, Tennessee

Charlie Gibbons, Ed.D.
Director, Youth and School Age
    Programs
Maxwell Air Force Base, Alabama
Former Adjunct Professor,
    Alabama State University
Health, Physical Education and
    Dance Department
Montgomery, Alabama

Jan Marie Ozias, Ph.D., R.N.
Former Director, Texas Diabetes
    Council; and Consultant, School
    Health Programs
Austin, Texas

Carl Anthony Stockton, Ph.D.
Dean, School of Education
The University of Texas at
    Brownsville and Texas
    Southmost College
Brownsville, Texas
Former Department Chair and
    Professor of Health Education
Department of Health and
    Applied Human Sciences
The University of North Carolina
    at Wilmington
Wilmington, North Carolina

Printed in the United States of America

ISBN 13: 978-0-15-355124-6
ISBN 10: 0-15-355124-0

1 2 3 4 5 6 7 8 9 10 032 15 14 13 12 11 10 09 08 07 06

Chapters

1 Your Amazing Body 2

2 Taking Care of Yourself 30

3 Food for a Healthy Body 58

4 Activity for a Healthy Body 84

5 Keeping Safe 106

6 Emergency Safety 124

7 Preventing Disease 144

8 Medicines and Other Drugs 170

9 Avoiding Tobacco and Alcohol 194

10 About Yourself and Others 214

11 Your Family and You 240

12 Health in the Community 258

Reading in Health Handbook 282

Health and Safety Handbook 294

Contents

Introduction to Health x
Life Skills xii
Building Good Character xiv
Reading in Health xvi

CHAPTER 1

Your Amazing Body 2

1 Bones, Muscles, and Nerves **4**
2 Breathing and Digestion **8**
3 You Grow and Change **14**
BUILDING GOOD CHARACTER
Respect **17**
4 People Grow at Different Rates **18**
LIFE SKILLS
Communicate **22**
5 Taking Care of Your Body **24**
Activities **27**
Chapter Review and Test Preparation **28**

CHAPTER 2

Taking Care of Yourself 30

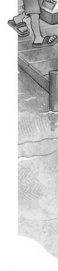

1 Your Skin **32**
2 Your Teeth and Gums **36**
BUILDING GOOD CHARACTER
Respect **41**
3 Your Ears, Eyes, and Nose **42**
4 Health-Care Products **46**
LIFE SKILLS
Set Goals **50**
5 Advertising **52**
Activities **55**
Chapter Review and Test Preparation **56**

CHAPTER 3 Food for a Healthy Body 58

1 Why Your Body Needs Food 60

2 MyPyramid 64

3 Healthful Foods 68

 BUILDING GOOD CHARACTER
Responsibility 71

4 Being A Wise Food Shopper 72

LIFE SKILLS
Make Responsible Decisions 76

5 Handling Food Safely 78

Activities 81

Chapter Review and Test Preparation 82

CHAPTER 4 Activity for a Healthy Body 84

1 Keeping Your Body Fit 86

BUILDING GOOD CHARACTER
Fairness 91

2 Staying Safe While Exercising 92

LIFE SKILLS
Make Responsible Decisions 98

3 Rest and Sleep for Health 100

Activities 103

Chapter Review and Test Preparation 104

CHAPTER 5

Keeping Safe 106

1 Being Responsible for Your Safety 108

 BUILDING GOOD CHARACTER
Responsibility 111

2 Safety Around Others 112

LIFE SKILLS
Resolve Conflicts 116

3 Safety On Wheels 118

Activities 121

Chapter Review and Test Preparation 122

CHAPTER 6

Emergency Safety 124

1 Safety Around Fire and Poisons 126

BUILDING GOOD CHARACTER
Citizenship 129

2 Home Safety 130

LIFE SKILLS
Communicate 134

3 Disaster Safety 136

Activities 141

Chapter Review and Test Preparation 142

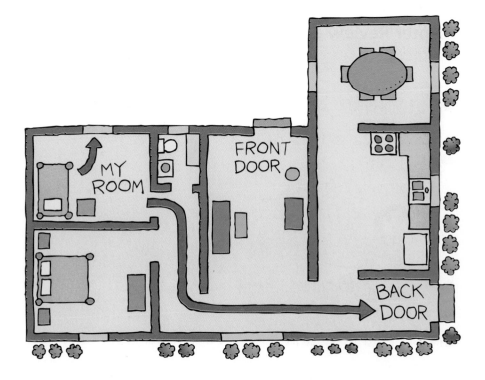

Preventing Disease **144**

1 Learning About Disease **146**

2 Diseases You Can Catch **148**

3 Fighting Disease **152**

 LIFE SKILLS
Manage Stress **156**

4 Diseases You Can't Catch **158**

BUILDING GOOD CHARACTER
Caring **163**

5 Staying Healthy **164**

Activities **167**

Chapter Review and Test Preparation **168**

Medicines and Other Drugs **170**

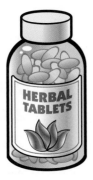

1 Learning About Drugs **172**

2 Using Medicines Safely **178**

BUILDING GOOD CHARACTER
Trustworthiness **181**

3 Harmful and Illegal Drugs **182**

 LIFE SKILLS
Refuse **186**

4 Say NO to Drugs **188**

Activities **191**

Chapter Review and Test Preparation **192**

Avoiding Tobacco and Alcohol **194**

1 Tobacco and Its Effects **196**

BUILDING GOOD CHARACTER
Trustworthiness **201**

2 Alcohol and Its Effects **202**

LIFE SKILLS
Refuse **206**

3 Refusing to Use Alcohol and Tobacco **208**

Activities **211**

Chapter Review and Test Preparation **212**

CHAPTER 10

About Yourself and Others 214

1 Understanding Your Feelings 216

2 Coping With Emotions 222

 LIFE SKILLS
Manage Stress 226

3 Relationships with Family and Friends 228

BUILDING GOOD CHARACTER
Caring 233

4 Communicating with Others 234

Activities 237

Chapter Review and Test Preparation 238

CHAPTER 11

Your Family and You 240

1 Learning About Families 242

BUILDING GOOD CHARACTER
Fairness 245

2 Changes in Families 246

LIFE SKILLS
Resolve Conflicts 250

3 Families Help Each Other 252

Activities 255

Chapter Review and Test Preparation 256

CHAPTER 12 Health in the Community 258

1 Where to Get Health Care 260

2 Keeping the Environment Healthful 264

★ BUILDING GOOD CHARACTER
Citizenship 267

3 Controlling Water Pollution 268

LIFE SKILLS
Set Goals 272

4 Reduce, Reuse, Recycle 274

Activities 279

Chapter Review and Test Preparation 280

Reading in Health Handbook 282

Compare and Contrast 282

Draw Conclusions 284

Identify Cause and Effect 286

Identify Main Idea and Details 288

Sequence 290

Summarize 292

Health and Safety Handbook 294

Glossary 308

Index 318

Why should you learn about health?

You can do many things to help yourself stay healthy and fit. Just as importantly, you can avoid doing things that will harm you. If you know ways to stay safe and healthy and do these things, you can help yourself have good health throughout your life.

Keeping clean

Eating right

Getting enough rest

Staying active

Why should you learn about life skills?

Being healthy and fit doesn't come from just knowing facts. You also have to think about these facts and know how to use them every day.

These are some important life skills for you to have:

Communicating

Sharing ideas, needs, and feelings with others

Making Responsible Decisions

Deciding the most responsible thing to do to avoid taking risks

Managing Stress

Finding ways to avoid and relieve negative feelings and emotions

Refusing

Saying *no* to doing things that are risky and dangerous

Setting Goals

Deciding on specific ways to make improvements to your health and fitness

Resolving Conflicts

Finding solutions to problems in ways that let both sides win

Whenever you see 🏃 LIFE SKILLS in this book, you can learn more about using life skills.

Why should you learn about good character?

Having good character is also an important part of having good health. When you have good character, you have good relationships with others and can make responsible decisions about your health and fitness.

These are some important character traits:

Caring

Showing kindness and concern for friends, family, and others

Citizenship

Having pride in your school and community and obeying rules and laws

Fairness

Treating others equally, playing by the rules, and being a good sport

Respect

Showing consideration for yourself and others

Responsibility

Doing what you are supposed to do, practicing self-control, and completing tasks

Trustworthiness

Being honest, dependable, and loyal

Whenever you see **Building Good Character** in this book, you can learn more about building good character.

What are ways to be a successful reader?

Students need good reading skills to do well in school. Here are some tips to help you understand, remember, and use information you read.

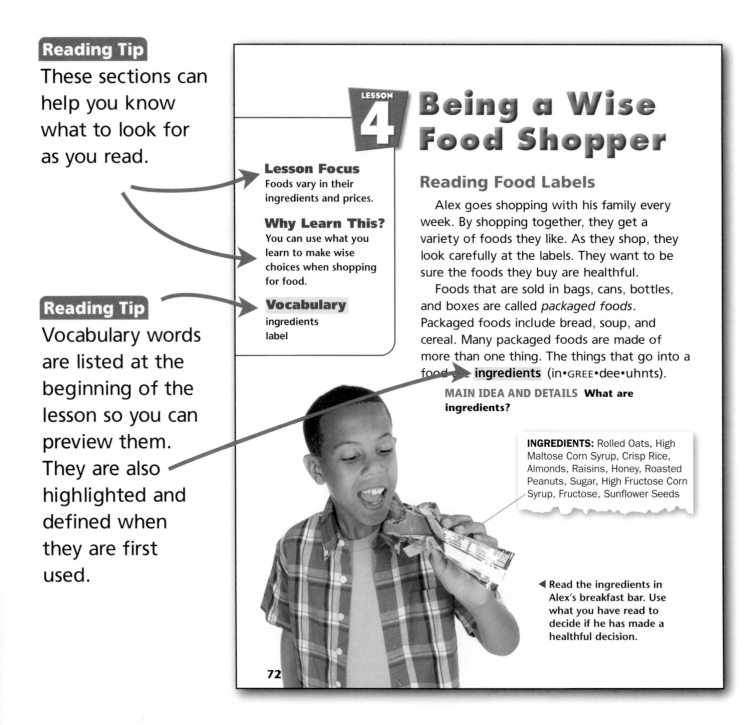

Reading Tip

These sections can help you know what to look for as you read.

Reading Tip

Vocabulary words are listed at the beginning of the lesson so you can preview them. They are also highlighted and defined when they are first used.

LESSON 4

Being a Wise Food Shopper

Lesson Focus
Foods vary in their ingredients and prices.

Why Learn This?
You can use what you learn to make wise choices when shopping for food.

Vocabulary
ingredients
label

Reading Food Labels

Alex goes shopping with his family every week. By shopping together, they get a variety of foods they like. As they shop, they look carefully at the labels. They want to be sure the foods they buy are healthful.

Foods that are sold in bags, cans, bottles, and boxes are called *packaged foods*. Packaged foods include bread, soup, and cereal. Many packaged foods are made of more than one thing. The things that go into a food are **ingredients** (in•GREE•dee•uhnts).

MAIN IDEA AND DETAILS **What are ingredients?**

INGREDIENTS: Rolled Oats, High Maltose Corn Syrup, Crisp Rice, Almonds, Raisins, Honey, Roasted Peanuts, Sugar, High Fructose Corn Syrup, Fructose, Sunflower Seeds

◀ Read the ingredients in Alex's breakfast bar. Use what you have read to decide if he has made a healthful decision.

72

Check your understanding by answering these questions at the end of each section. These questions also help you practice reading skills. You will see six reading focus skills:

► Compare and Contrast
► Draw Conclusions
► Identify Cause and Effect
► Identify Main Idea and Details
► Sequence
► Summarize

Whenever you see 🌟(Focus Skill) in this book, you can learn more about using reading skills.

Use this section to summarize what you have read, review vocabulary and concepts, and practice writing skills.

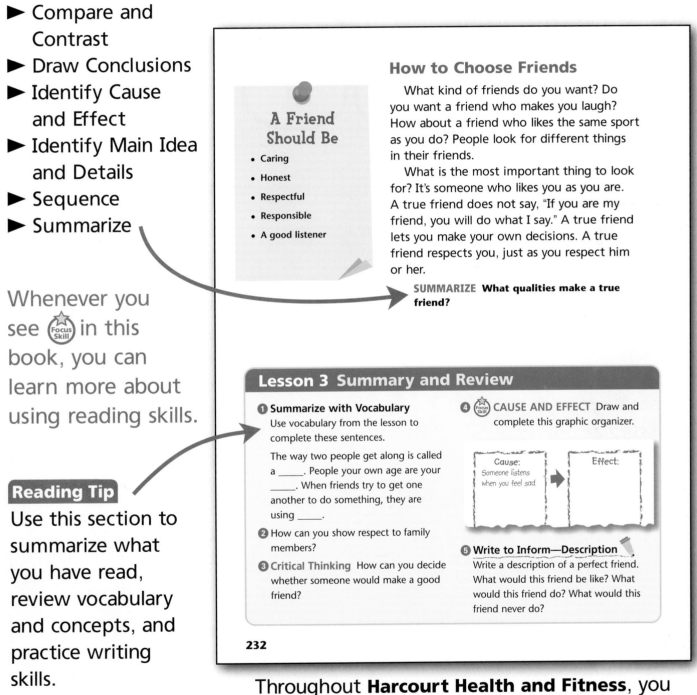

A Friend Should Be

• Caring
• Honest
• Respectful
• Responsible
• A good listener

How to Choose Friends

What kind of friends do you want? Do you want a friend who makes you laugh? How about a friend who likes the same sport as you do? People look for different things in their friends.

What is the most important thing to look for? It's someone who likes you as you are. A true friend does not say, "If you are my friend, you will do what I say." A true friend lets you make your own decisions. A true friend respects you, just as you respect him or her.

SUMMARIZE What qualities make a true friend?

Lesson 3 Summary and Review

1 Summarize with Vocabulary
Use vocabulary from the lesson to complete these sentences.

The way two people get along is called a _____. People your own age are your _____. When friends try to get one another to do something, they are using _____.

2 How can you show respect to family members?

3 Critical Thinking How can you decide whether someone would make a good friend?

4 🌟CAUSE AND EFFECT Draw and complete this graphic organizer.

| Cause: Someone listens when you feel sad. | → | Effect: |

5 Write to Inform—Description
Write a description of a perfect friend. What would this friend be like? What would this friend do? What would this friend never do?

232

Throughout **Harcourt Health and Fitness**, you will have many opportunities to learn new ideas and skills that will lead to good health.

Your Amazing Body

IDENTIFY MAIN IDEA AND DETAILS
The main idea is the most important thought in the text you have read. Details tell about the main idea. Use the Reading in Health Handbook on pages 288–289 and this graphic organizer to help you learn the health facts in this chapter.

Identify Main Idea and Details

Main Idea:

Detail: | Detail: | Detail:

Health Graph

INTERPRET DATA It takes between twenty-three and thirty-three hours for a meal to move through your whole digestive system. In which part of the digestive system does food spend the most time? In which part does it spend the least time?

Time Food Spends in Each Part of the Digestive System

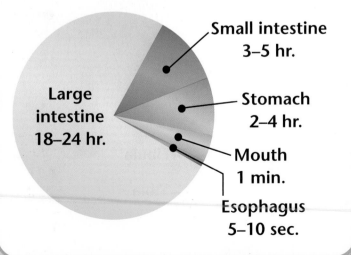

Small intestine
3–5 hr.

Large intestine
18–24 hr.

Stomach
2–4 hr.

Mouth
1 min.

Esophagus
5–10 sec.

Daily Physical Activity

Exercising will help keep all of your body systems healthy.

🎵 *Be Active!*
Use the selection **Track 1, Saucy Salsa**, to get your whole body moving.

Bones, Muscles, and Nerves

Your Skeletal System

Your **skeletal system** is made up of all the bones in your body. A **bone** is a strong, hard body part. If you didn't have bones, you wouldn't be able to stand, sit, or play.

Bones have different shapes and sizes. Round bones in your back help you stand up. Wide, flat bones in your head protect your brain. Long bones in your legs help you move.

You can help keep your skeletal system strong by exercising and by getting enough calcium. Calcium is a mineral in foods such as milk, cheese, and yogurt.

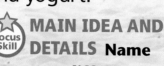 **MAIN IDEA AND DETAILS Name two different kinds of bones and what they do for your body.**

Skull

Ribs

Spine

Pelvis

Femur

Fibula

Tibia

Your Muscular System

Your muscular system is made up of muscles. A **muscle** (MUH•suhl) is a body part that causes movement. Tendons attach muscles to bones. A **tendon** is a strong strip of tough material.

To move your body parts, muscles often work in pairs. For example, one muscle pulls to raise your arm. Another muscle pulls to lower it. Your muscles let you do many kinds of activities. You can walk, run, and throw a ball. With practice, you can do smaller movements such as writing, painting, and playing an instrument.

SUMMARIZE What is the main job of your muscles?

Flexor

Pectoral

Abdominal

Quadricep

Flexor

Did You Know?

Babies have more bones than adults do. At birth, a baby has more than 300 bones. As a person grows, some bones grow together. An adult has only 206 bones.

Your Nervous System

Your **brain** is your body's control center. The brain gets messages from other parts of the body. First, the brain decides what to do with the information. Next, the brain sends messages to other parts of the body. **Nerves** carry messages to and from the brain. Some messages go through the **spinal cord**, nerves that run through the backbone. The messages tell the body what to do.

You can protect your nervous system by wearing proper safety gear. When you ride in a car, wear your safety belt. When you bike or skate, wear a helmet.

SEQUENCE What does your brain do first when it receives a message from your body?

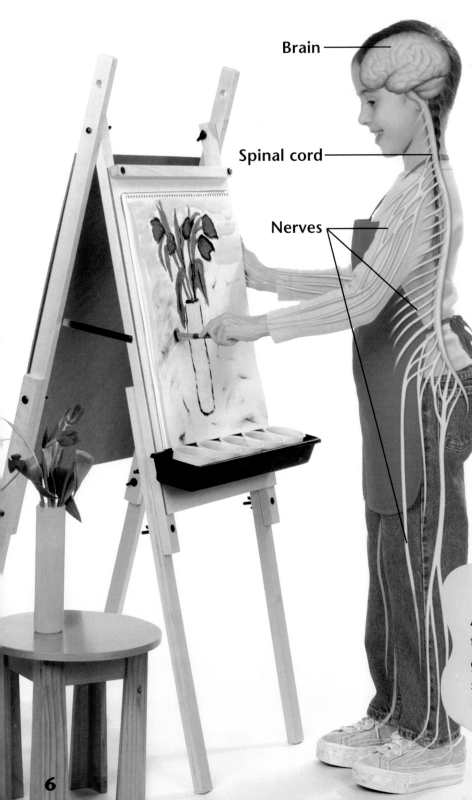

Brain

Spinal cord

Nerves

Quick Activity

Analyze Pictures List two messages that the girl's brain might be sending to her body.

6

Systems Work Together

Think about what happens when you run to catch a ball. First, your brain sends a message to your leg muscles, telling them to move. Then the muscles pull on your leg bones to make your legs move. As you run, your brain sends and receives many other messages. Your nervous, skeletal, and muscular systems work together for you to catch the ball.

DRAW CONCLUSIONS Suppose someone throws a ball at you. What happens if your brain doesn't send the message to your muscles?

This boy is using his muscular, skeletal, and nervous systems to play the piano. ▶

PERSONAL HEALTH PLAN ▶

Real-Life Situation
To play the piano, you need good control of your muscles.

Real-Life Plan
Write a plan for how you could improve your muscle skills.

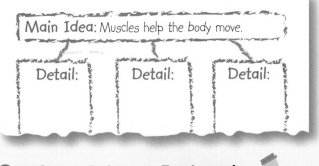

Lesson 1 Summary and Review

❶ Summarize with Vocabulary
Use vocabulary from this lesson to complete the statements.

Your _____ is made of strong, hard body parts called _____. Nerves, bones, and _____ work together to move body parts. A _____ connects a muscle to a bone. The _____ sends messages to muscles to make them move.

❷ Name one way to keep your nervous system healthy.

❸ Critical Thinking Give one example of how body systems work together.

❹ (Focus Skill) MAIN IDEA AND DETAILS Draw and complete this graphic organizer to show the main idea and details.

Main Idea: Muscles help the body move.

Detail: Detail: Detail:

❺ Write to Inform—Explanation
Explain the way the brain sends messages through the body.

Breathing and Digestion

Your Respiratory System

When you breathe in, air passes through your *nose* and *mouth*. The air moves into your **trachea** (TRAY•kee•uh), a tube that connects your throat to your lungs.

Your **lungs** are the main parts of your respiratory system. Oxygen (AHK•si•juhn) gas from the air moves through the walls of the lungs to all parts of your body. A gas called carbon dioxide (KAR•buhn dy•AHK•syd) is made by your body. This gas moves from the rest of your body into your lungs. The carbon dioxide leaves the body in the air that you breathe out.

Your **diaphragm** (DY•uh•fram) is a thin, flat muscle under your ribs. The diaphragm moves to help move air into and out of your lungs.

You can keep your respiratory system healthy by exercising and getting enough rest. Staying away from tobacco smoke can also help keep your respiratory system healthy.

SEQUENCE What happens to the air you take in through your nose and mouth?

◀ Your respiratory system is always working, no matter what you are doing.

▼ Blowing this horn is only one way this boy uses his respiratory system.

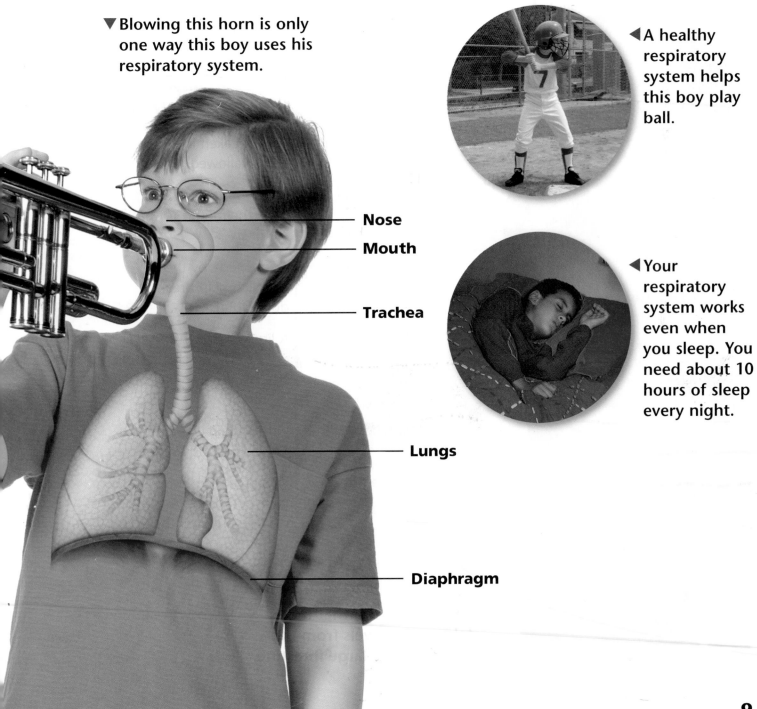

◀ A healthy respiratory system helps this boy play ball.

Nose

Mouth

Trachea

◀ Your respiratory system works even when you sleep. You need about 10 hours of sleep every night.

Lungs

Diaphragm

How Your Systems Work Together

The parts of your body work together like the parts of a car. Each part of a car is important to help it run. Each of your body systems also has an important job in helping you move, grow, and live. Your skeletal system protects your body parts the same way a car's frame protects the people inside the car.

Your nervous system is like the driver of the car. The driver controls the car just as your brain controls messages to your body.

▼ For this car to move, all the parts must work together.

The driver also keeps the car working by taking care of the parts of the car. You can help keep your body working by staying healthy.

DRAW CONCLUSIONS A car needs gasoline for fuel. What is the fuel for your body?

▼ To stay healthy, your body parts must work together like a team.

Lesson 2 Summary and Review

❶ Summarize with Vocabulary
Use vocabulary from this lesson to complete the statements.

Air moves from the nose and mouth to the _____ and into the _____. Food moves from the mouth through the _____ and into the _____. Next, the food goes into the small _____. The _____ collects waste.

❷ What are two ways you can keep your respiratory system healthy?

❸ Critical Thinking Name two jobs of the digestive system.

❹ (Focus Skill) MAIN IDEA AND DETAILS
Draw and complete this graphic organizer. List three details for the main idea given.

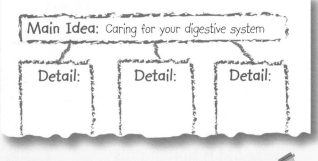

Main Idea: Caring for your digestive system

Detail: | Detail: | Detail:

❺ Write to Entertain—Short Story
Write a funny story about how an apple might "feel" as it is being eaten.

13

You Grow and Change

The Human Life Cycle

Almost anywhere you go, you see people of different ages. They include babies, children, adults, and seniors. The human **life cycle** is made up of four stages of growth that people go through.

Birth to Two Have you ever been around a baby? If so, you know that babies are not able to take care of themselves. They can't walk or talk, and they must be cared for to stay alive. By age two, a child is more active and more independent.

Birth to Two
A person grows faster between birth and age two than at any other time in life. This two-year-old is holding his new baby sister.

Two to Ten Between ages two and ten, your mind and body grow a great deal. You are able to learn many things, such as how to speak, read, and write. Your body grows about two or three inches a year.

Ten to Adult At about age ten or twelve, you will start changing into an adult. As a teenager, you might grow about four or five inches in one year. Your body will become heavier, too. Girls usually begin this growth stage before boys, but boys soon catch up. Your body will grow and change when the time is right for you.

Adult to Senior When you are an adult, you'll stop growing taller. But the bodies of adults continue to change in other ways.

COMPARE AND CONTRAST How are the first two stages in the life cycle alike and different?

Ten to Adult
How do you think you will look when you are twenty?

Adult to Senior
Adults and seniors enjoy many of the same activities.

15

How You Have Changed

It's hard to believe you were once a tiny baby! You couldn't hold up your head. You had to cry to let someone know you were hungry. An adult had to take care of you.

Since then, your body and your mind have grown a lot. Before you were two, you could hold up your head, sit up, and crawl. Later, you learned to walk and talk.

Now you can read, write, and solve problems. You can do many things that you couldn't do as a baby.

CAUSE AND EFFECT You can read and solve problems. What is the cause of this effect?

Lesson 3 Summary and Review

❶ Summarize with Vocabulary

Use vocabulary and other terms from this lesson to complete the statements.

The four stages of growth are part of the human _____. People grow the fastest before age _____. From ages two to _____, children learn how to do harder tasks. Sometime after the age of ten, you begin to change from a child into an _____.

❷ What skills do you learn during your second stage of growth?

❸ Critical Thinking Why do you think seniors, or older adults, have different needs than children?

❹ (Focus Skill) **MAIN IDEA AND DETAILS**

Draw a graphic organizer like this with four detail boxes. Show the four stages of the human life cycle and a detail about each stage.

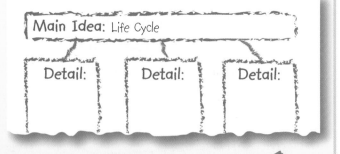

Main Idea: Life Cycle

Detail: Detail: Detail:

❺ Write to Inform—Description

Write a paragraph about how your life will be different when you are an adult.

Respect

Showing Respect for Adults

Respect is something that all people deserve. When you treat other people with respect, it makes them feel good. It also makes you feel good. Here are some ways that you can show respect for people older than you, especially senior adults.

- **Always use proper language. Use "sir" and "ma'am" when talking to adults.**
- **Saying "please" and "thank you" shows people that you respect what they are doing for you.**
- **Offer to give up your seat to an adult in a waiting area or on a bus, train, or subway.**
- **Don't interrupt while others are speaking.**
- **When an adult speaks, listen politely and carefully.**
- **Answer questions politely.**

Activity

With a parent, visit an elderly neighbor or a retirement home. Ask the person you are visiting to tell about himself or herself at your age. Use the tips above as you speak and listen.

People Grow at Different Rates

How People Grow

Your body grows when cells in your body multiply, or make more cells. A **cell** is the smallest working part of your body. Your body makes new cells to replace old or dead cells and to provide growth.

Your bones, brain, and muscles are all made of cells. Cells have the information your body needs to work well.

SUMMARIZE Explain why cells are important.

Quick Activity

Interpret Graphs
These students are the same age but are growing at different rates. At home, make a graph showing the heights of the students. Show your own height on the graph, too.

Rates of Growth

Third-Grade Students

Nerve cell

Each type of cell in your body does a special job. ▶

Bone cells

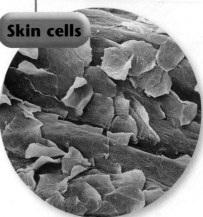

Skin cells

What Cells Do

Cells have different shapes and sizes to carry out different jobs in your body. Nerve cells are long and have branches on their ends. The ends help the nerve cells send messages. Bone cells make a hard material that makes bones strong. Skin cells are flat and form layers to protect your body.

A group of cells that work together to do a certain job is called a **tissue**. One kind of tissue is muscle tissue. When different groups of tissues work together to do a certain job, they are called an **organ**. Your heart is an organ that pumps blood to all parts of your body. An **organ system** is a group of organs that work together to do a job.

DRAW CONCLUSIONS Why do you think the body has cells of different shapes and sizes?

Did You Know?

The surface of your skin is made up of twenty-five to thirty layers of dead skin cells. These layers protect the living cells under them.

The Special Way You Grow

As your cells multiply, you grow physically. As your bones get longer, you grow taller. As your muscles get larger, you become stronger. You are able to run faster and throw a ball farther. You also add weight to your body as you grow.

Each person's growth rate is different. Your **growth rate** is how quickly or slowly you grow. You have read that before age two, your growth rate was very fast. At your age now, your growth rate has slowed down some. It will get faster again when you are a teenager.

Your classmates may be taller, shorter, bigger, or smaller than you. You may worry that you are growing too quickly or too slowly. Remember that you are growing at the rate that is right for you.

As you grow physically, you grow in mental ways, too. *Mental* means "of the mind." As you grow, the nerve cells in your brain get bigger. When you learn, these cells connect with other brain cells. They make pathways. Your brain builds new pathways as you continue to learn new things.

The Growing Tree

Welcome to the Growing Club

You are learning how to do things that are more difficult. You can probably ride a bike. Maybe you can even play a musical instrument. Your thinking skills have improved. You can also solve harder problems and make decisions. You are more able to take care of yourself.

SUMMARIZE Explain why you should not worry about your growth rate.

Health & Technology

Doctors sometimes look at the inside of the body when they are trying to find out why a person is hurt or ill. Sometimes they use an X ray to see what bones look like. At other times, they use magnetic resonance imaging (MRI) to see what organs look like.

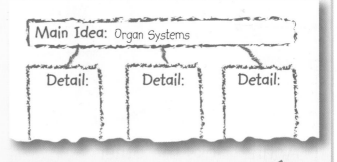

An open MRI ▶

Lesson 4 Summary and Review

❶ **Summarize with Vocabulary**

Use vocabulary from this lesson to complete the statements.

The smallest working part of your body is called a _____. A group of cells that work together to do a job is a _____. The lungs are examples of an _____. The respiratory system is an example of an _____.

❷ What happens as your cells multiply?

❸ **Critical Thinking** Describe the two ways your body grows.

❹ (Focus Skill) **MAIN IDEA AND DETAILS**

Draw and complete this graphic organizer.

Main Idea: Organ Systems

Detail: Detail: Detail:

❺ **Write to Inform—Explanation**

Explain some of the ways you have grown mentally in the last five years.

21

Communicate
Your Feelings

Using "I" messages can help you explain your feelings. "I" messages use *I* to tell how you feel, such as, "I feel happy when we all get along." Knowing the steps for **Communicating** can also help you talk about your feelings.

Angie feels left out and uncomfortable because she is taller than the other girls and boys in her class. What can Angie do to feel better?

1 Understand your audience.

Angie thinks the other students are ignoring her because she is tall.

2 Give a clear message.

Angie uses "I" messages to tell the others her feelings about being taller than they are.

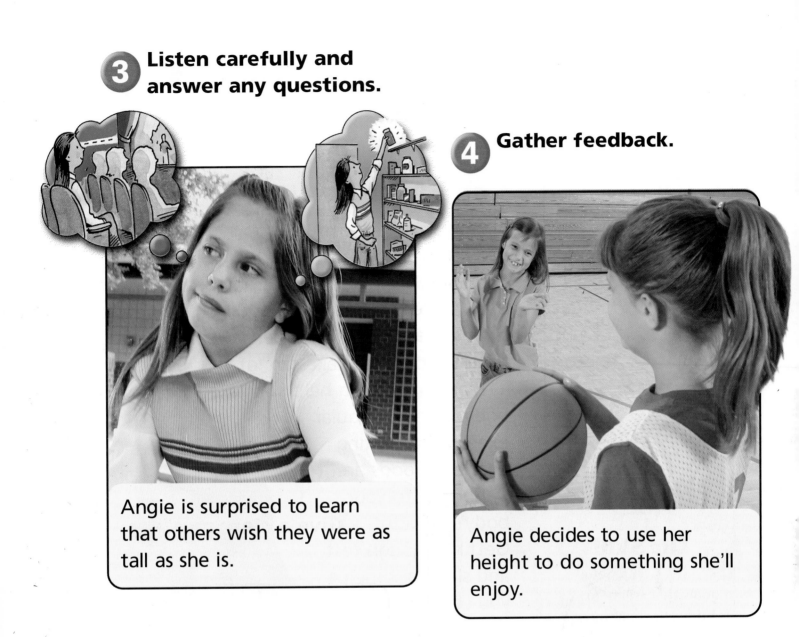

3 Listen carefully and answer any questions.

Angie is surprised to learn that others wish they were as tall as she is.

4 Gather feedback.

Angie decides to use her height to do something she'll enjoy.

Problem Solving

Robert is in the third grade. He has a new baby brother who needs a lot of attention. He wants to help his parents by watching over his baby brother. How can Robert **communicate** to his parents that he is responsible enough to look after his brother?

Taking Care of Your Body

Lesson Focus

Taking good care of your body helps you grow in healthy ways.

Why Learn This?

Use what you learn to develop good health habits.

Vocabulary

private

Life Skills

Set Goals Set two goals that will help your body stay healthy. How can you work each day to meet these goals?

Good Health Habits

Do you eat healthful foods every day? Do you brush your teeth twice a day? These are habits that help keep your body healthy. A *habit* is something you do so often, you don't have to think about it. When you practice good health habits, you take care of your body.

Many habits can help you take care of your body. Getting regular exercise and eating healthful foods are important to your body's growth. Getting enough rest and sleep also helps you stay healthy.

These students are helping their teacher by putting up posters to remind themselves and others of healthful habits. ▶

Wash your hands
Soap

Keep your body, hair, nails, and teeth clean, and wash your hands often. These habits help remove dirt from your body. Dirt contains germs that can make you sick.

Cooperating during regular checkups is important, too. Your doctor can check how you are growing. Your dentist can help you take care of your teeth.

Another good habit is wearing proper safety gear. It can protect your body from getting hurt.

DRAW CONCLUSIONS What might happen if you eat with dirty hands?

Quick Activity

Make Posters
The students' posters show only some of the ways to keep you healthy. Make two more posters that show how you can keep your body healthy.

Good Touches and Bad Touches

There are likely some things you don't wish to share. It might be a diary or a picture you drew. Everyone has things that are **private**, or things that belong only to that person. Everyone should respect the privacy of others.

Just as some objects are private, some parts of your body are private. Good touches, like getting a hug from someone you trust, may make you feel good. However, bad touches can hurt you or make you feel afraid or uncomfortable. If someone touches you in a bad way, do these things:

- Tell the person to stop.
- Get away from the person.
- Tell a trusted adult, such as a parent, a teacher, a nurse, or a doctor.

▼ This grandmother is giving a good touch.

MAIN IDEA AND DETAILS Give an example of a good touch.

Lesson 5 Summary and Review

1 Summarize with Vocabulary
Use vocabulary and another term from this lesson to complete the statements.

Something you don't want to share with others is _____. A pat on the back by someone you trust is a _____ touch.

2 Critical Thinking Why is taking good care of your body important?

3 Who can you talk to if someone makes you feel uncomfortable?

4 MAIN IDEA AND DETAILS Draw and complete this graphic organizer. Show the main idea and details.

Main Idea: Ways to care for your body

Detail: Detail: Detail:

5 Write to Entertain—Poem
Write a funny poem about a make-believe student who never takes a bath.

26

ACTIVITIES

Language Arts

Write a Story Write a short story about a four-year-old who wishes he were as tall as his ten-year-old brother. Describe the problems he might have being taller than others his age.

Science

Compare Life Cycles Find out about the life cycles of other living things, such as butterflies or frogs. How are their stages of growth similar to the stages in the human life cycle? How are they different?

Technology Project

Use a camera to take photos of people who are at different stages of the human life cycle. Display the photos in a poster. Write captions to explain what each photo shows.

 For more activities, visit The Learning Site.
www.harcourtschool.com/health

Home & Community

Communicating Interview older family members about jobs they did when they were your age. Which jobs are the same as the ones you do now? Which are different?

Career Link

Pediatrician A pediatrician is a doctor who takes care of babies and children. Suppose you are a pediatrician with a seven-year-old patient who refuses to eat fruit. Write what you would say to help the patient change his or her eating habits.

Reading Skill

MAIN IDEA AND DETAILS

Draw and use this graphic organizer to answer questions 1 and 2.

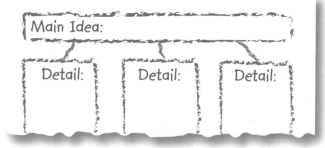

Main Idea:

Detail: Detail: Detail:

1 Fill in the stages of the human life cycle.

2 Fill in the parts of the digestive system.

Use Vocabulary

Match each term in Column B with its meaning in Column A.

Column A	Column B
3 A strong, hard body part	**A** nerves
	B growth rate
4 A body part that enables bones to move	**C** bone
	D lungs
5 Cells that carry messages	**E** muscle
6 Main organs of the respiratory system	
7 How quickly or slowly you grow	

Check Understanding

8 Your nervous system is made up of your nerves, your brain, and your _____. (p. 6)

A lungs   **C** stomach

B spinal cord   **D** muscles

9 A gas you breathe out is _____. (p. 8)

F lungs   **H** oxygen

G carbon dioxide   **J** trachea

10 Which body system helps break down your food? (p. 10)

A digestive system

B muscular system

C respiratory system

D nervous system

11 Which part of a car is like your skeleton? (p. 12)

F

H

G

J

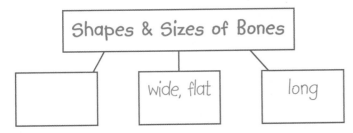

Shapes & Sizes of Bones

| | wide, flat | long |

12 Which term is missing from this graphic organizer? (p. 4)

A little   **C** short

B round   **D** small

13 Which of these systems is **NOT** used to catch a ball? (p. 7)

F skeletal   **H** nervous

G muscular   **J** digestive

14 In which part of the human life cycle would you be most likely to learn how to ride a bike? (p. 15)

A birth to two

B two to ten

C ten to adult

D adult to senior

15 The tough tissue that attaches muscles to bones is _____. (p. 5)

F nerve   **H** tendon

G cell   **J** organ

Think Critically

16 Suppose your lungs could not do their job of getting oxygen into the body properly. How would this affect how you feel and your everyday activities?

17 When a baseball bat is broken in half, it remains in two pieces. When a bone is broken, bone cells make repairs. Tell why a bat cannot repair itself, but a bone can repair itself.

Apply Skills

18 **BUILDING GOOD CHARACTER**
Respect You are at a friend's house for dinner. Your friend's mom asks you some questions. List one way that you can show respect for her as you communicate.

19 **LIFE SKILLS**
Communicate You and a friend are going skating. You know you should both wear a helmet, but your friend doesn't want to. Use an "I" message to communicate that you want to be responsible by wearing a helmet.

Write About Health

20 **Write to Inform—How-To** Suppose you have a friend who does not know how to ride a bicycle. Make a list of the skills and steps needed to ride a bike.

Taking Care of Yourself

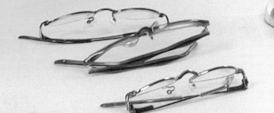

Reading Skill

SUMMARIZE To summarize you briefly restate the main idea and the most important details and tell how they are connected. Use the Reading in Health Handbook on pages 292–293 and this graphic organizer to help you read the health facts in this chapter.

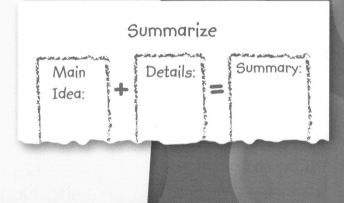

Health Graph

INTERPRET DATA Your skin covers your entire body. Skin isn't the same thickness at all parts of the body. Where is skin the thickest? Where is it the thinnest?

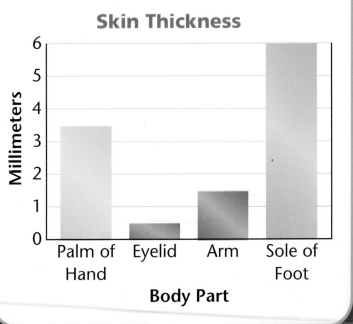

Daily Physical Activity

Exercising is one way to take care of yourself.

Be Active!
Use the selection **Track 2**, **Locomotion**, to take care of your muscles and bones.

Your Skin

LESSON

1

Keeping Your Skin Clean

Lesson Focus

Caring for your skin helps you stay healthy.

Why Learn This?

You can use what you learn to practice good skin care.

Vocabulary

pores
bacteria
sunscreen

Look carefully at the skin on your arm. What do you see? You might see some tiny hairs. Oil comes up through the skin along these hairs. The oil helps keep your skin soft.

You probably can't see them, but your skin also has tiny holes. These holes are called **pores**. Sweat comes to the surface of the skin through the pores. Sweating helps cool your body. That's why you sweat when you get hot.

▼ You should wash your hands several times a day.

Oil, sweat, and dirt collect on your skin. Bacteria grow on your skin, too. **Bacteria** (bak•TIR•ee•uh) are living things that are too tiny to see. Some bacteria cause illness. Washing with soap and warm water is the best way to get rid of things that collect on your skin.

Washing your hands often is important. Clean hands are less likely to spread colds and other illnesses. Here are some times when you should wash your hands:

- before you eat
- after using the bathroom
- after coughing or blowing your nose
- after touching an animal

To clean your whole body, take a bath or a shower. Use plenty of soap. Some people need to bathe every day. Bathe whenever you are dirty or sweaty.

 SUMMARIZE Why is washing your skin important to your health?

Quick Activity

When Do You Need Sunscreen? List at least three activities you like to do where you would need to wear sunscreen.

Protecting Your Skin from the Sun

The sun warms you and gives you light. But too much sun can harm your body. The sun gives off harmful rays. These rays can burn your skin. This is called a sunburn. A sunburn seems to go away in a few days. However, the real harm from too much sun might show up years later. Skin cancer can grow where you once had a sunburn. Skin cancer is very dangerous. Some kinds can kill you.

The sun is strongest in the middle of the day. It's best to stay out of the sun between 10:00 A.M. and 4:00 P.M.

▼ Sun protection is important even when you are in the shade.

◄ Long sleeves and long pants will help protect you from the sun. On hot days, choose loose, light-colored clothes that are light in weight.

Rub sunscreen on all uncovered skin. ▶

If you must go out in the sun, cover up and use sunscreen. **Sunscreen** can protect you from the sun's harmful rays. You need sunscreen not only in the summer but also anytime you are in the sun. Ask an adult to help you choose a sunscreen that is right for you.

Put on a sunscreen of SPF 30 or higher thirty minutes before going outside. Reapply sunscreen every two hours. Additional sunscreen may be needed if you are sweating or swimming.

The sun's rays can hurt your eyes, too. Wear sunglasses and a hat to protect your eyes. Never look right at the sun, even when you are wearing sunglasses.

CAUSE AND EFFECT What harmful effects on the skin can be caused by the sun?

Myth and Fact

Myth: A tan is a sign of good health.

Fact: There is no such thing as a "healthful tan." A tan means your skin has been burned by the sun's harmful rays.

Lesson 1 Summary and Review

❶ Summarize with Vocabulary

Use vocabulary and other terms from this lesson to complete the statements.

Your skin has many _____, or tiny holes, in it. _____ comes out of these holes to help cool off your body. Living things, called _____, collect on the skin and may cause illness. You can protect your skin from the sun's rays by using _____.

❷ List three times when you should wash your hands.

❸ Critical Thinking Why must even young children avoid sunburns?

❹ (Focus Skill) SUMMARIZE Draw and complete this graphic organizer to summarize ways to keep your skin healthy and safe.

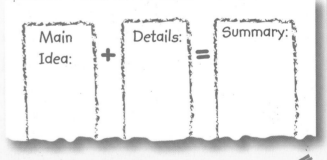

❺ Write to Express—Friendly Letter
Your friend is going to join you for a vacation at the beach. Write your friend a letter telling how to protect his or her skin while on the beach.

Your Teeth and Gums

Lesson Focus

You can take good care of your teeth and gums by learning how to floss and brush and how to protect your teeth from injury.

Why Learn This?

Caring for your teeth and gums helps you stay healthy.

Vocabulary

plaque
cavity
dental floss
fluoride

Some Things That Can Harm Teeth and Gums

Your teeth help you bite and chew. They help you talk, and they make your smile look good. You probably still have some of your primary teeth. Some of your permanent teeth may grow in this year. These teeth can last for the rest of your life if you take care of them.

A sticky material called **plaque** (PLAK) can build up on your teeth. Plaque contains bacteria that break down tiny bits of food and form acids.

These acids can make a hole in the tooth called a **cavity** (KAV•ih•tee). A cavity damages a tooth.

This boy's healthy teeth help him look good and feel good about himself.▶

36

A cavity begins in the enamel. Over time, the cavity can grow through the dentin and the pulp. If that happens, the tooth becomes very painful, and it may die.

Plaque that stays on a tooth gets hard. It can build up and make your gums weak. If the gums get very weak, teeth may fall out.

Missing teeth can often be replaced, but it's much better to keep your own teeth healthy. Regular checkups by a dentist can help prevent tooth problems. So can keeping your teeth clean.

Focus Skill **SUMMARIZE Describe how a cavity forms.**

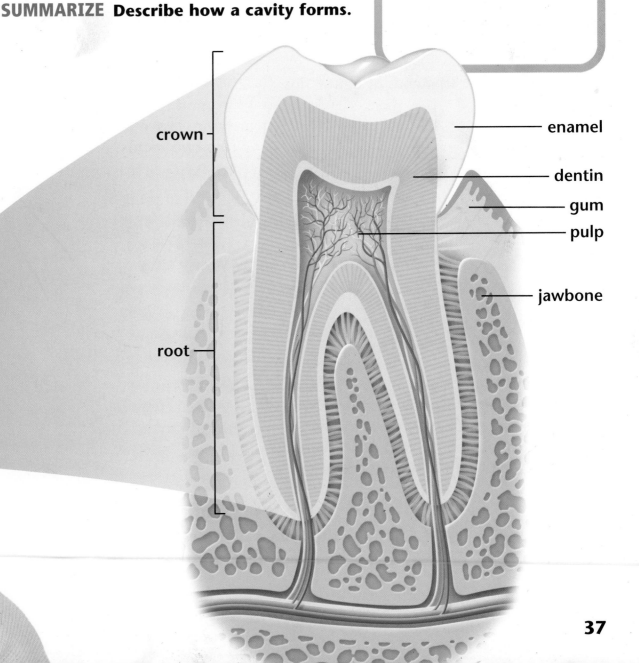

crown

root

enamel

dentin

gum

pulp

jawbone

Flossing Your Teeth

To floss, you need a special thread called **dental floss** . Flossing removes plaque and food from between your teeth. Floss at least once a day. Here's how.

1. Pull out about 18 inches of dental floss.

2. Wrap one end of the piece of floss around the middle finger of each hand. Leave a few inches between the two hands.

3. Use your thumbs and index fingers to guide the floss. Gently push it between two teeth. Rub gently up and down away from the gum. Rub near the gum line of one tooth and then the other.

4. Remove the floss. Unwind it a bit to reach a clean part. Repeat for each tooth in your mouth.

DRAW CONCLUSIONS Why should you unwind the floss a bit to reach a clean part before moving on to another tooth?

▲ Brush your teeth at least twice a day. Brushing in the morning removes bacteria that grew while you slept.

▲ Brush your teeth carefully before bedtime to remove any bits of food.

Brushing Your Teeth

Brush your teeth to remove food and loosened plaque. Use a soft-bristle toothbrush. Soft bristles will clean your teeth without hurting your gums. Some toothpastes have fluoride. **Fluoride** (FLAWR•eyed) is a chemical that makes teeth stronger and harder. Strong, hard teeth are less likely to get cavities.

Brush with short, back-and-forth movements on all of your teeth. Brush along the gum line and across your tongue. Spend extra time on your back teeth. They have deep pits where plaque can collect. Turn your toothbrush to reach the inner sides of your teeth. When you finish brushing, spit out the toothpaste. Rinse your mouth with water.

Personal Health Plan ▶

Real-Life Situation
Your teeth should last your entire lifetime.

Real-Life Plan
Make a plan for how you will take care of your teeth each day.

Focus Skill
SUMMARIZE Why should you use a toothbrush with soft bristles?

Protecting Your Teeth

Always protect your teeth. Don't use them for cutting or tearing things other than food. Wear a mouth guard during sport activities to protect your teeth from being hit or injured.

If a tooth gets knocked out, a dentist may be able to save it. If the tooth is dirty, first rinse it lightly in a little milk or water. Put the tooth back in, hold it in place, and go right to a dentist.

SEQUENCE If a tooth gets knocked out, what should you do first, next, and last?

Wear a mouth guard if you play any sport or participate in any activity, in which your mouth could be injured. ▶

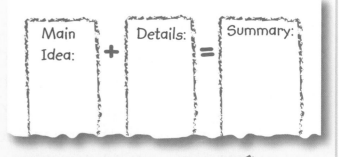

Lesson 2 Summary and Review

❶ **Summarize with Vocabulary**

Use vocabulary and other terms from the lesson to complete the statements.

The sticky coating that forms on teeth is called _____. Use _____ to remove food between teeth. Brush your teeth at least _____ a day. Protect your teeth during sports by wearing a _____.

❷ How can bacteria harm teeth?

❸ **Critical Thinking** Why is brushing along your gum line important?

❹ **SUMMARIZE** Draw and complete this graphic organizer. In the first two boxes tell ways to keep your teeth and gums healthy. Then write a summary in the last box.

Main Idea:	+	Details:	=	Summary:

❺ **Write to Inform—How-To**

Write a radio announcement telling people how to floss and brush.

Self-Respect

Good Grooming

Good grooming helps you look neat and clean. By using good grooming habits, you show that you have respect for yourself. You also show that you have respect for other people. Here are some rules for good grooming.

- **Keep your body clean by taking a bath or shower.**
- **Wash your face with soap and warm water.**
- **Wash your hair at least twice each week or when it gets dirty or sweaty. Keep your hair neatly combed.**
- **Wash your hands frequently with soap and warm water. Scrub your nails and keep them trimmed.**
- **Brush and floss your teeth every day.**
- **Wear clothing that is clean and neat.**
- **Check yourself in a mirror to make sure you look your best.**

Activity

Make a daily grooming checklist. Ask family members to add other grooming tips. Use the checklist before you leave the house each day.

Your Ears, Eyes, and Nose

Lesson Focus

Learning about your ears, eyes, and nose can help you take good care of them.

Why Learn This?

Caring for your ears, eyes, and nose helps you stay healthy.

Vocabulary

ear canal
eardrum

Protecting Your Ears

Sound waves enter your ear at the opening to the **ear canal**. At the end of the ear canal is the **eardrum**. The sound waves cause your eardrum to vibrate, or move back and forth. These movements are picked up by nerves that send signals to your brain, and you hear sound.

Quick Activity

Identify Noises The pictures show some things that make noises that can harm your ears. List at least four other loud noises that might harm your ears.

Loud sounds can harm your ears. They may cause you to have trouble hearing. Bacteria can cause an ear infection. If you have an infection, you may have pain in your ear and you may have trouble hearing. If this happens, tell a parent or another trusted adult. You may need medicine from a doctor.

You can avoid some of the things that might hurt your ears. Stay away from noisy places. Turn the sound down when you listen to music or the TV. When you use headphones, make sure you can still hear sounds around you.

Clean the outer parts of your ears with a washcloth. Never put anything inside your ear canal. Doing this could make a hole in your eardrum and damage your hearing.

MAIN IDEA AND DETAILS Give three details that tell how you can protect your ears.

▲ Getting hit on your ears can harm your hearing. Wear a helmet when you play sports such as football, baseball, and hockey.

Personal Health Plan ▶

Real-Life Situation
Suppose one of your chores is to help your mom with the yard.

Real-Life Plan
Make a list of ways you can protect your ears and eyes while doing your chores.

Protecting Your Eyes

Your eyes are important parts of your body. You should always take good care of them. If you have blurry vision, pain, or trouble seeing, tell a parent or teacher right away.

One way your eyes can be harmed is by the sun's rays. Wearing sunglasses can help protect your eyes. When you do activities that might harm your eyes, protect them by wearing safety glasses. These activities include playing some sports, mowing the grass, and using paints. Also, have your eyesight checked about every two years by a doctor.

MAIN IDEA AND DETAILS **Write two details that support the main idea of this section.**

◀ This girl and her dad are wearing safety glasses because the tools they are using might harm their eyes.

44

Protecting Your Nose

Although your nose is not as easily hurt as your eyes and ears, you still need to take care of it. Taking care of your nose is very important when you have a cold.

Always blow your nose gently. Keep both nostrils and your mouth open. If you blow your nose too hard, air pressure pushes your eardrum and can cause ear pain.

Blowing your nose too hard also can break blood vessels. When that happens, your nose may bleed. Follow the tips on this page for stopping a nosebleed.

SEQUENCE If you have a nosebleed, what is the next step after, tilt your head forward and look down?

▼ If you get a nosebleed, stand or sit up. Tilt your head forward and look down. Gently pinch the soft part of your nose. Breathe through your mouth.

Lesson 3 Summary and Review

❶ Summarize with Vocabulary

Use vocabulary and other terms from this lesson to complete the statements.

Sound enters the ear through the _____. The _____ moves back and forth when sound waves hit it. _____ sounds can harm your ears. You should protect your eyes from the sun by wearing _____. Taking care of your nose is very important when you have a _____.

❷ Critical Thinking Why should you **NOT** put anything into your ears?

❸ What are three activities that you do for which you should wear safety glasses?

❹ (Focus Skill) SUMMARIZE Draw and complete this graphic organizer. In the center box, write a detail on how to protect your hearing. Then write a summary in the box on the right.

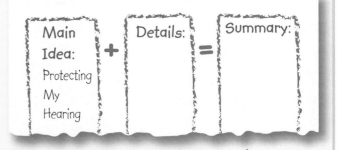

Main Idea: Protecting My Hearing + Details: = Summary:

❺ Write to Inform—How-To

Write a list of things you would tell a younger brother or sister about how to care for his or her eyes, ears, and nose.

Health-Care Products

Learning About Health-Care Products

Products people buy to take care of themselves are health-care products. These include soap, shampoo, and toothpaste.

As you get older, you will have more responsibility for buying health-care products. You will learn to make good buying decisions.

A person who chooses or buys products is a **consumer**. Just about everyone is a consumer.

 SUMMARIZE In what ways are you a consumer?

Did You Know?

Just because a famous person tells you a product is good doesn't mean it is. People who make products pay famous people to say good things about their products.

▼ Shampoo is only one product you use as a consumer.

Reading Health-Care Product Labels

The first step in buying a product is to decide if it's something you need or something you want. You don't need everything you want to buy. Sometimes it's okay to buy something that you just want to have. Knowing why you want to buy something can help you make the right decision about buying.

Next, you must choose which product is best for you. Read the label to help you make the best choice. Labels give you important information about a product. They tell what the product is made of and how to use it.

SEQUENCE **What is the first step in deciding whether to buy a product?**

▼ Read all of the label before you use a product. Make sure you show a trusted adult the directions before you use any product.

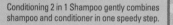

Conditioning 2 in 1 Shampoo gently combines shampoo and conditioner in one speedy step.

Ophthalmologist-Tested Formula is tear-free and easy on eyes.

Extra Conditioning eliminates tough tangles and tames even thick and curly hair.

DIRECTIONS: Wet hair, squeeze a quarter size amount into palm, apply to hair, lather and rinse well.

CAUTION: FOR EXTERNAL USE ONLY. KEEP OUT OF THE REACH OF YOUNG CHILDREN EXCEPT UNDER ADULT SUPERVISION.

INGREDIENTS: Water (Aqua), Sodium Trideceth Sulfate, PEG-80 Sorbitan Laurate, Cocamidopropyl Hydroxysultaine, Disodium Lauro-amphodiacetate, PEG-150 Distearate, Sodium Laureth-13 Carboxylate, Polysorbate 20, Glycerin, Polyquaternium-10, Citric Acid, Tetrasodium EDTA, DMDM Hydantonin, Fragrance (Parfum), Methylchloroisothia-zolinone, Methylisothiazolinone, D&C Red No. 33 (CI 17200).

Bottle made with 25% recycled plastic. Bottle coded for recycling. Check if facilities exist.

DIRECTIONS
Apply to wet hair and rub gently. Rinse completely.

CAUTION
Keep out of eyes. If shampoo does get into eyes, rinse with clear water.

INGREDIENTS
Have a parent or another trusted adult check the ingredients to see if you are allergic to any of them.

Comparing Health-Care Products

Different products may not look or smell exactly the same. But many have the same main ingredients. Ingredients are the things the product is made of. You can find out what a product's ingredients are by reading its label. Some brands of a health-care product may have the same ingredients, but their prices may be different. Look at the graph. It shows the prices of five shampoos. They all have the same main ingredients. Each has the same amount of shampoo, 12 ounces. How do their prices compare?

Quick Activity

Each shampoo has the same ingredients for cleaning hair. Which shampoo offers the best deal?

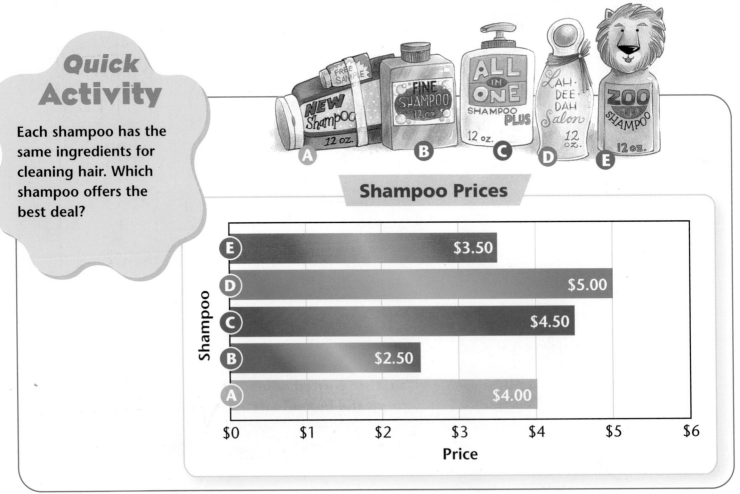

Shampoo Prices

48

Some products have added ingredients that might make the product smell different from or do more than other products. For example, the All in One Shampoo has ingredients to reduce tangles. The products with extra ingredients sometimes cost more than products without them.

Most often, you should buy the item that costs the least and meets your needs. Only the consumer can decide which product is best for him or her. Knowing how to make buying decisions will help you make the best choice.

COMPARE AND CONTRAST How are the shampoos shown the same and different?

Myth and Fact

Myth: It is always best to buy a large bottle of a product.

Fact: Larger sizes are not always a better deal. A large size may cost more per ounce. You may not need the larger size. Buy only as much as you need.

Lesson 4 Summary and Review

❶ Summarize with Vocabulary
Use vocabulary and other terms from this lesson to complete the statements.

Everyone who buys products is a _____. To choose health-care products, you should _____ products. Important information is found on the product _____. The _____ are the things the product is made of.

❷ Critical Thinking Why should you compare products before you buy?

❸ Who should read the ingredients of a health-care product before you use it?

❹ (Focus Skill) SUMMARIZE Draw and complete this graphic organizer. Write the main idea and two details you can learn from a label.

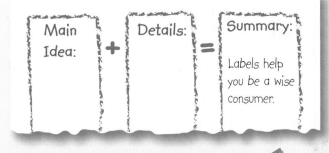

Main Idea: + Details: = Summary: Labels help you be a wise consumer.

❺ Write to Inform—Explanation
Suppose you are going to buy some soap. Explain how to decide which soap is best for you.

49

Set Goals

For Choosing Health-Care Products

You make choices about health-care products all the time. Using the steps for **Setting Goals** can help you make healthful choices when you buy health-care products.

Matt visited the dentist and learned he has a cavity in one tooth. He wants to avoid more cavities. What should Matt do?

1 Choose a goal.

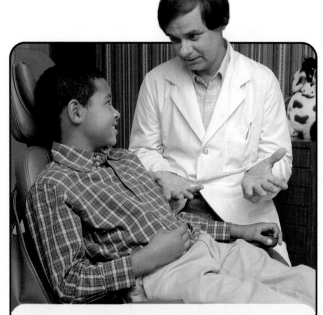

Matt already brushes and flosses his teeth. His dentist tells him to use a toothpaste that contains fluoride to make his teeth stronger.

2 List and plan steps to meet the goal. Determine whether you will need help.

Matt writes a plan and then goes to the store with his mother. There, they will choose a toothpaste with fluoride.

Matt checks the labels of several toothpastes to find one that has fluoride.

His goal was to get a toothpaste with fluoride. He succeeded in reaching his goal.

Problem Solving

Melissa wants to be able to go to the swimming pool often during the summer. Her mother is worried about how being in the sun so much might affect Melissa's skin. Melissa has decided to develop a plan to show her mother she can safely be in the sun.

Use the steps for **Setting Goals** to help Melissa make a plan to go to the pool often. Tell how Melissa's plan would show she is taking responsibility for her health.

Advertising

Types of Advertising

Advertising is a way companies tell consumers about products. Advertisements, or ads, try to get people to buy products. Advertising is found in all types of *media*, such as television, radio, newspapers, magazines, and the Internet. It is even found on buses, subways, and taxis.

Some of the information in ads is good. But some ads can mislead you. At times companies will try to get you to buy a product by paying a famous person to say good things about their product.

Lesson Focus

Advertising can give good information, but it can trick you, too.

Why Learn This?

Knowing how to analyze advertising messages can make you a better consumer.

Vocabulary

advertising

Consumer Activity

Analyze Media Messages Some ads make offers that seem great. Then fine, or small, print in the ad tells you the full story. Find an example of an ad with fine print. Explain how the offer in the ad isn't what it seems to be.

52

Some companies use ads that make you think you will be "cool" if you use their product. The ads show pictures of happy-looking people using the product. Some ads use catchy tunes to get your attention.

Advertisers also use packaging to get you to buy. They might use bright colors or pictures that people will notice. Some companies use popular movie characters. Knowing the tricks advertisers use can help you make better buying decisions.

SUMMARIZE **What is the main goal of advertising?**

Drink **Jolly Juice**

Start your day the Jolly way! Drink Jolly Juice!

Quick Activity

Locate Ads List all the ways Jolly Juice is being advertised. Then add to the list other places you have seen ads.

Responsibility Paulo is going to buy a new toothbrush. He says that he saw his favorite athlete in an ad for that toothbrush. How can Paulo find out if the ad gives the facts he needs? How will this help him make a responsible decision?

Be a Responsible Consumer

As a consumer, you are responsible for choosing the products you buy and use. Where can you get good information about health-care products?

Your parents and other adult family members can help you find out about a product. Professionals such as doctors and pharmacists are also good sources of information.

You can check the information in consumer magazines and on government websites. Ask a media specialist or librarian for help. Never use the Internet without adult supervision.

DRAW CONCLUSIONS How can you find out the facts about a product?

Lesson 5 Summary and Review

❶ Summarize with Vocabulary
Use vocabulary and other terms from this lesson to complete the statements.

_____ is a way companies tell about their products and try to get people to buy them. Knowing the facts about ads can help you make better buying _____. It is your _____ to find out the facts about products you buy.

❷ Why should you not always believe everything you read in an ad?

❸ Critical Thinking Why do companies spend money to make advertisements?

❹ (Focus Skill) SUMMARIZE Draw and complete this graphic organizer. Write ways advertisers try to get you to buy.

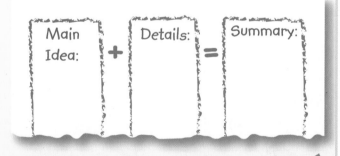

Main Idea: + Details: = Summary:

❺ Write to Express—Business Letter
Write a letter to a company that makes shampoo. Ask for information about the product. Explain why you want to know.

Math

Calculate Tooth Growth The large, flat teeth in the back of your mouth are called molars. Three sets of permanent molars grow in as you age. One set grows in about every six years. About how old will you be when your third set grows in?

Science

Observe Skin With a hand lens, look at the skin on your hands. Do you see dirt, dry skin, or other things? Now wash your hands carefully. Look at your skin again with the hand lens. Compare what you see with what you observed on your unwashed hands.

Technology Project

Use a video camera to make five daily health news reports, or use a computer to make slide presentations. In each report, tell how to take care of the eyes, ears, or skin. Each day, show one report to your class.

For more activities, visit The Learning Site.
www.harcourtschool.com/health

Home & Community

Analyze Ads With a family member, look at five advertisements in newspapers or magazines or on TV. Together, decide how each ad tries to get people to buy the product.

Career Link

Audiologist An audiologist is a health-care worker who tests people's hearing. Some audiologists sell hearing aids to people who need them. Suppose you are an audiologist. Write an ad that encourages people to protect their ears and their hearing.

Reading Skill

SUMMARIZE

Draw and use this graphic organizer to answer questions 1 and 2.

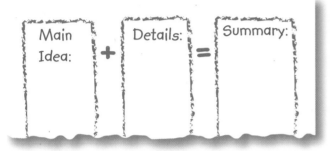

Main Idea: + Details: = Summary:

1 Write two things to do each day to keep your teeth and gums healthy.
2 Write two ways to protect your skin.

Use Vocabulary

Complete each sentence with a word from the chapter.

3 Sweat comes to the surface of the skin through holes called _____.

4 Companies use _____ to convince you to buy something.

5 Sound waves cause your _____ to move back and forth.

6 You can protect your skin against the sun's harmful rays by using _____.

7 A _____ is a person who chooses or buys products.

Check Understanding

Choose the letter of the correct answer.

8 Where would you find information about how to use a health-care product? (p. 47)
A on the product label
B in the product advertising
C in a newspaper
D in an encyclopedia

9 For which sport might you **NOT** need to wear a mouth guard? (p. 40)
F baseball   H basketball
G swimming   J soccer

10 Which shows a good way to avoid spreading germs? (p. 33)

A 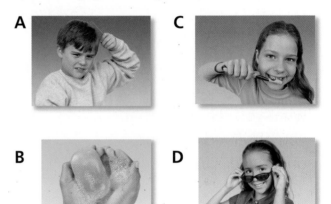   C

B   D

11 The hard surface of a tooth is the _____. (p. 37)
F root   H pulp
G dentin   J enamel

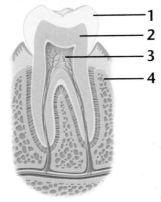

12 Which number shows the enamel? (p. 37)

A 1   **C** 3

B 2   **D** 4

13 You can protect your eyes from the sun's harmful rays by _____. (p. 35)

  F using sunscreen

  G wearing sunglasses

  H going out in mid afternoon

  J wearing safety glasses

14 Which can cause a cavity in a tooth? (p. 37)

  A acids from bacteria in plaque

  B small pieces of dental floss

  C food that isn't completely chewed

  D tearing a package with your teeth

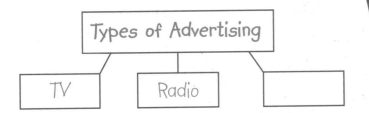

15 Which does **NOT** belong in the graphic organizer? (pp. 52–53)

  F billboard

  G newspaper

  H window sign

  J textbook

Think Critically

16 Why might someone who seldom washes his or her hands be likely to get or spread an infection?

17 Why should you floss even if you brush twice a day?

Apply Skills

18 **BUILDING GOOD CHARACTER**
Self-Respect You have been invited to a friend's house for a birthday party. Apply what you know about showing respect for yourself and others to describe how you will get ready for the party.

19 **LIFE SKILLS**
Set Goals You are going on a winter vacation, and you will be outside in the sun and snow most of the day. Show that you are responsible while on vacation by using the steps for setting goals to protect your skin and eyes.

Write About Health

20 **Write to Inform—Explanation**
Explain how each consumer can show responsibility for his or her health.

3 Food
for a
Healthy Body

Reading Skill

COMPARE AND CONTRAST When you compare, you tell how two or more things are alike. When you contrast, you tell how they are different. Use the Reading in Health Handbook on pages 282–283 and this graphic organizer to help you read the health facts in this chapter.

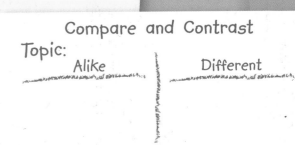

Compare and Contrast

Topic: _____

Alike	Different

Health Graph

INTERPRET DATA People were asked which picnic food they like the best: grilled hot dogs, grilled hamburgers, grilled chicken, or barbecued ribs. Which food was chosen the most often?

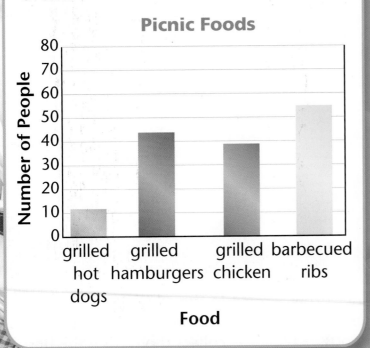

Picnic Foods

Number of People / Food

Daily Physical Activity

Eating the correct foods can give you energy for physical activities.

Be Active!
Use the selection **Track 3, Late for Supper,** to use some food energy.

Why Your Body Needs Food

Where Food Comes From

Many of the foods we eat come from plants. Fruits and vegetables come from plants. So do beans, nuts, seeds, and grains.

When plants are ripe, they are harvested. Some fruits and vegetables are sold fresh, while others are sent to factories to be canned or frozen and packaged.

Other foods people eat come from animals. Many people eat meat from cows, sheep, pigs, chicken, and fish. Most of our eggs come from chickens, and most of our milk comes from cows.

COMPARE AND CONTRAST How are meats and vegetables alike and different?

◀ Cranberries grow on shrubs or vines in bogs.

▲ In the early fall, when the cranberries are ripe, farmers collect them from the bog.

Why Food Is Important

Food gives your body energy to grow and be active. **Nutrition** (noo·TRISH·uhn) is the study of food and how it affects your body. Understanding nutrition can help you stay healthy.

Nutrients (NOO·tree·uhnts) are the things in food that help your body grow and get energy. There are six basic nutrients. They are carbohydrates, proteins, fats, vitamins, minerals, and water. All these nutrients can be found in the foods we eat every day. Different kinds of food have different nutrients.

SUMMARIZE Why is food important for your body?

Health & Technology

Food Freshness Scientists are working on new ways to show the freshness of some foods. Spoiling foods give off gases. The gases can change the color of a special dot. This dot can be put into a package of food. When the dot changes color, the shopper will know that the food is no longer safe to eat.

▲ Trucks take the juice from the factory to the store, where your family can buy it.

▲ After they are collected, the cranberries are taken to the factory.

100% Juice

all natural
Cranberry Juice

Nutrients in Foods

The foods you eat and drink make up your **diet** (DY•uht). Most people can get almost all the nutrients they need by eating different kinds of foods.

Fats

Fats give your body more energy than any other nutrient. Energy your body doesn't use right away is stored as fat. Later, your body can use that fat for energy. Fats can be found in butter, oil, cheese, nuts, and whole milk.

Proteins

Proteins (PROH•teenz) also give your body energy. They help your body grow. Proteins can be found in foods such as meat, fish, eggs, chicken, milk, and nuts.

Carbohydrates

Carbohydrates (kar•boh•HY•drayts) give your body energy. They can be found in bread, pasta, and fruit. They can also be found in some vegetables such as carrots, peas, and corn.

Vitamins

Vitamins (VY•tuh•minz) are nutrients that help your body do different jobs. For example, vitamin A helps keep your skin and eyes healthy. It can be found in carrots, tomatoes, and broccoli. Oranges provide vitamin C.

Minerals

Minerals (MIN•uhr•uhlz) are nutrients that help your body grow and work. Milk contains calcium. Spinach contains calcium and iron. Bananas have potassium. Fluoride is needed for strong teeth. It's often added to tap water.

Water

Your entire body needs water in order to work properly. There is a lot of water in foods such as celery, watermelon, and pineapple. However, you need to drink a lot too.

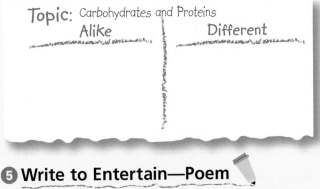

DRAW CONCLUSIONS Why is it important for you to include many different kinds of foods in your diet?

Lesson 1 Summary and Review

1 Summarize with Vocabulary
Use vocabulary from this lesson to complete the statements.

Understanding _____ will help you know how food affects your body. You should choose different foods to get all the _____ you need to grow, stay active, and keep healthy. The foods you eat are part of your _____.

2 Critical Thinking Why do you think it is important to group foods by the nutrients they contain?

3 Name six nutrients. Give an example of a food that contains each nutrient.

4 Focus Skill COMPARE AND CONTRAST
Draw and complete this graphic organizer to show how proteins and carbohydrates are alike and different.

Topic: Carbohydrates and Proteins

Alike	Different

5 Write to Entertain—Poem
Write a poem about the importance of nutrients.

MyPyramid

A Way to Choose Foods

A **food guide pyramid** (PEER•uh•mid) is a tool to help you choose foods for a healthful diet. The United States Department of Agriculture (USDA) has made its own food guide pyramid, called MyPyramid. **MyPyramid** shows which foods to eat each day to stay healthy. The pyramid also encourages people to be active. Activities such as walking, running, biking, dancing, doing yard work, and playing sports keep you physically active.

A **balanced diet** is a diet made up of a healthful amount of foods from each of the food groups. Using MyPyramid can help you plan a balanced diet.

 Focus Skill COMPARE AND CONTRAST What is alike and different between MyPyramid and a balanced diet?

Grains

Vegetables

Fruits

Milk

Meat and Beans

Real-Life Situation
Suppose you want a more healthful diet.
Real-Life Plan
List all the foods you eat for one day. Compare your list with the food groups shown in MyPyramid. List the foods that you could add to make your diet balanced.

Your Daily Diet

MyPyramid organizes healthful foods into five groups. The groups are shown by stripes. Grains make up the widest stripe. The largest part of your daily diet should come from the Grains group. The thinnest stripe is oils. Oils are not a group, but the body needs oils in small amounts.

Choosing foods from each group is only the first step in building a balanced, healthful diet. You need to choose a variety of foods from within each group. You also need to choose the right portions, or amounts of each food. How can you do that? The tables on these pages show you how.

Making Good Food Choices

Food Group	Recommendations
Grains	At least half of the grains you eat should be whole grains. Choose whole wheat and rye bread, brown rice and pasta, and oats.
Vegetables	Eat lots of dark green vegetables such as spinach and broccoli and orange vegetables such as carrots and squash, Eat fewer starchy vegetables such as potatoes and corn. Include a selection of other vegetables such as tomatoes and mushrooms.
Fruits	Eat fresh fruits such as apples, oranges, berries, bananas, grapes, and melons. Limit the amount of fruit juice you drink. It can contain a lot of sugar. If you do drink juice, choose one that is 100 percent juice.
Oils	Get your oils from foods such as nuts, olives, fish, and avocados, and from liquid oils. Try to limit the oils you get from butter and margarine.
Milk	Milk products include milk and foods made from milk that keep their calcium, such as cheese and yogurt. Foods made from milk that have little or no calcium, such as butter and cream cheese, are not included. Choose milk products that are low in fat or fat-free.
Meat and Beans	Eat fish, nuts, and seeds more often than meat or poultry. When you do eat meat and poultry, cut off all the fat you can see and take off the skin.

Estimating Portions

Food Group	Daily Portion	Easy Estimates
Grains	5 ounces	An ounce equals one slice of bread, an ice cream scoop of cooked rice, oats, or pasta, or a fistful of cereal flakes.
Vegetables	$1\frac{1}{2}$–2 cups	A cup is about the size of a baseball, a fist, or two ice cream scoops.
Fruits	$1\frac{1}{2}$ cups	A cup is about the size of a baseball, a fist, or two ice cream scoops.
Oils	4–5 teaspoons	A teaspoon is about the size of a penny or a fingertip.
Milk	2–3 cups	A cup is about the size of a baseball, a fist, or two ice cream scoops.
Meat and Beans	4–5 ounces	An ounce of beans would fill an ice cream scoop. A 3-ounce portion of cooked meat, fish, or poultry is about the size of a computer mouse.

= 1 cup

= 3 ounces

= 1 teaspoon

= 1 ounce

(Focus Skill) **COMPARE AND CONTRAST How are the Fruits group and the Vegetables group the same and different?**

Lesson 2 Summary and Review

1 Summarize with Vocabulary
Use vocabulary from this lesson to complete the statements.

The USDA developed ____ to help you choose foods to eat for a healthful diet. Choosing foods from each food group will help you eat a ____.

2 What are the five food groups in MyPyramid?

3 Critical Thinking Why do you think the Milk group has a wider stripe than the Fruits group?

4 (Focus Skill) COMPARE AND CONTRAST
Draw and complete this graphic organizer.

Topic: Oils and Grains
Alike   Different

5 Write to Inform—How-To
Write three steps you could take to plan a healthful, balanced menu for one day, using MyPyramid.

Healthful Foods

Healthful Meals

A potato is rich in carbohydrates, vitamins, and minerals. But if you ate only potatoes, meal after meal, day after day, you would not be healthy. In fact, you could get sick. Potatoes are healthful, but they do not contain all the nutrients you need.

No single food contains everything you need to stay healthy. That is why you need to eat balanced meals that include a variety of foods. Eating a variety of healthful foods will give you the energy you need to grow and stay active.

DRAW CONCLUSIONS
What might happen to you if you ate the same food at every meal, every day of the year?

Roberto's favorite breakfast is juice and cereal with milk. The graph shows how many times he had his favorite breakfast during the last four weeks. ▼

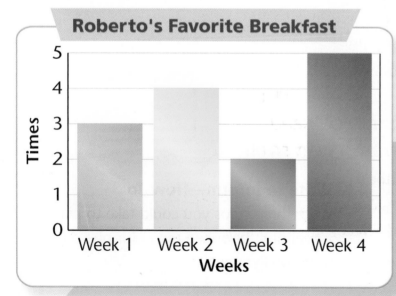

Roberto's Favorite Breakfast

cheese and whole-wheat crackers

grapes

carrots and celery

unbuttered popcorn

YOGURT
light n healthy
Strawberry
YOGURT

yogurt

Healthful Snacks

Snacks are foods you eat between meals. They can give you energy and keep you from getting too hungry. Healthful snacks can give you nutrients you might not get during meals.

As you use MyPyramid to choose foods, remember to include healthful snacks in your diet. A plum or a pear gives you a fruit serving. A granola bar gives you a serving from the Grains group. Some snacks are not healthful. Foods that are fried or have a lot of sugar don't give you the nutrients you need most. You should eat these foods only in small amounts or on special occasions.

Focus Skill **COMPARE AND CONTRAST How are healthful snacks and unhealthful snacks alike and different?**

Quick Activity

Choosing Healthful Snacks Decide which snack in the pictures you would choose. Which food group is your snack from? Explain why your snack choice is healthful. Then prepare and try the healthful snack at home.

Choosing Healthful Snacks

Asha wants a crunchy snack. Her popcorn counts as a serving from the Grains group. ▼

When you choose a snack, think about the nutrients it will give your body. Remember that healthful snacks do not contain a lot of fats, oils, or sugar. Decide on what type of snack you want. Are you hungry for a cold or sweet snack? Here are some ideas for healthful snacks to prepare and try.

- fresh fruit
- whole-grain cereal
- whole-wheat crackers
- unbuttered popcorn

- raw vegetables
- cheese
- raisins
- low-fat yogurt

CAUSE AND EFFECT Describe how you might feel if you eat a healthful snack rather than an unhealthful snack.

Lesson 3 Summary and Review

1 Summarize with Vocabulary

Use vocabulary and other terms from this lesson to complete the statements.

You should choose healthful _____ to eat between meals. They can give you _____ and keep you from getting too hungry. They can also give you _____ you might not get during meals. Use _____ to make healthful choices.

2 Name three healthful snacks you like to eat. Write if the snack comes from an animal or a plant.

3 Critical Thinking Why is it important to choose healthful snacks?

4 (Focus Skill) **COMPARE AND CONTRAST**

Draw and complete this graphic organizer to show how a snack of fruit and a snack of chocolate are alike and different.

Topic: Fruit and Chocolate Snacks

Alike	Different

5 Write to Inform—Explanation

Write a letter to an adult family member explaining why he or she should eat healthful snacks. Include suggestions for five healthful snacks that you would eat.

Responsibility

Eating a Healthful Lunch

You can show responsibility by keeping your body as healthy as possible. One way to stay healthy is by choosing healthful foods. Here are some simple rules for you to use when deciding on healthful lunches.

- **Check MyPyramid.**
- **Choose foods you enjoy.**
- **Choose healthful drinks including water.**
- **Choose foods that are fresh.**
- **Eat a variety of foods.**
- **Choose foods that give your body energy.**
- **Don't let friends or classmates talk you into making unhealthful choices.**

Activity

Take responsibility for eating a healthful lunch every day for a week. Sometimes this might be hard when you see your friends eating chips and cookies. Try to remember these foods are not needed every day. Using the list above can help you make healthful choices. Notice how you feel after lunch and between meals each day. Write about how it feels to be responsible by choosing to eat a healthful lunch.

Being a Wise Food Shopper

Reading Food Labels

Alex goes shopping with his family every week. By shopping together, they get a variety of foods they like. As they shop, they look carefully at the labels. They want to be sure the foods they buy are healthful.

Foods that are sold in bags, cans, bottles, and boxes are called *packaged foods*. Packaged foods include bread, soup, and cereal. Many packaged foods are made of more than one thing. The things that go into a food are **ingredients** (in•GREE•dee•uhnts).

MAIN IDEA AND DETAILS What are ingredients?

INGREDIENTS: Rolled Oats, High Maltose Corn Syrup, Crisp Rice, Almonds, Raisins, Honey, Roasted Peanuts, Sugar, High Fructose Corn Syrup, Fructose, Sunflower Seeds

◀ Read the ingredients in Alex's breakfast bar. Use what you have read to decide if he has made a healthful decision.

Ingredients
chicken stock, enriched egg noodles, carrots, water, salt, margarine, onion powder, garlic, and spice.

Ingredients
enriched egg noodles, salt, sugar, chicken meat, chicken fat, chicken flavoring, and onion.

Nutrition Facts
Serving Size 3 tbsp (20g) (makes 1 cup prepared)
Servings Per Container 6

Amount Per Serving
Calories 80   Calories from F

% Daily V

Total Fat 2g
  Saturated Fat 0.5g
Cholesterol 20mg
Sodium 690mg
Total Carbohydrate 11g
  Sugars less than 1g
Protein 3g

Iron 4%   •   Thiamin 15%
Riboflavin 6% • Niacin 8%
Folic Acid 6%

Not a significant source of dietary fiber, vitamin A, vitamin C and calcium.

*Percent Daily Values are based on a 2,000 calorie diet. Your daily values may be higher or lower depending on your calorie needs.
                    Calories   2,000   2,500
Total Fat   Less than   65g   80g
Sat Fat   Less than   20g   25g
Cholesterol   Less than   300mg   300mg
Sodium   Less than   2,400mg 2,400mg
Total Carbohydrate   300g   375g
  Dietary Fiber   25g   30g

ritrition Facts
Size 1/2 cup (123 g)
gs about 2.5
es 60
Cal. 20

t Per Serving   % DV*

Fat 2 g   3%
turated Fat 0 g   0%
esterol 5 mg   2%
um 900 mg   38%
al Carbohydrate 8 g   3%
Dietary Fiber 1 g   4%
Sugars 0 g
Protein 3 g

Vitamin A   6%
Vitamin C   0%
Calcium   0%
Iron   2%

* Percent Daily Values (DV) are based on a 2,000 calorie diet.

DIRECTIONS FOR USE
STOVE TOP: EMPTY CONTENTS INTO SAUCEPAN. SLOWLY STIR IN 1 CAN OF WATER. HEAT ON MEDIUM HEAT, STIRRING OFTEN. DO NOT BOIL.

MICROWAVE: EMPTY CONTENTS INTO MICROWAVE-SAFE BOWL. STIR IN 1 CAN OF WATER. COVER. MICROWAVE ON HIGH FOR 3 MINUTES OR UNTIL HEATED.

PROMPTLY REFRIGERATE ANY UNUSED PORTION IN A SEPARATE CONTAINER.

Comparing Food Products

Corn might be the only ingredient in a box of frozen corn. Other packaged foods, such as soup, bread, and frozen pizza, are made of many ingredients.

Every packaged food has a **label** that lists the ingredients in the food. The ingredients are listed in order of amount. The food found in the greatest amount is listed first. The food found in the least amount is listed last.

Food labels also have a list of nutrition facts that tell about the nutrients in the food. They show you how much of each nutrient is in the food. This information is important because similar foods are not the same. Similar foods can have different ingredients and different amounts of each nutrient.

DRAW CONCLUSIONS **How can a food label help you choose the most healthful packaged foods?**

Quick Activity

Comparing Soups
Compare the ingredients in the canned and dried chicken noodle soups. What are the two main ingredients in each soup? Which soup would you choose? Why?

ACTIVITY

Life Skills
Set Goals Brenda wants to choose more healthful snacks. Name one goal she can set to help her choose snacks that give her nutrients she needs. Name one goal she can set to stop her from choosing snacks that are not healthful.

Comparing Prices

Consumer Activity

Analyze Advertising and Media Messages
Some ads use "tricks" to get you to buy a product. Find an ad for a popular drink, such as a juice or a sports drink. Figure out what "tricks" the ad might be using to get you to buy the drink.

One kind of food can have many different prices. Some foods cost more because they carry brand names. You know them from ads. Instead of brand names, some foods have the store's name on them. These foods are *store brands* and are usually less expensive.

A small carton of juice costs less than a large carton. But the juice in a small carton might actually be more expensive. To find out which is more expensive, look at how much each one costs by weight, volume, or number. This is called the *unit price*. In most cases, the unit price of juice in a small carton is higher than the unit price of juice in a large carton. You can usually find the unit price on a tag near the food.

SUMMARIZE How can you find the best deal when you are shopping for a food?

▲ Orange juice comes in many different packages and sizes.

74

Making the Best Choice

To shop wisely, you need to compare products. Remember that two similar foods can contain different ingredients and different nutrients. Reading the food labels will help you decide which package contains the ingredients you want and the ingredients you don't want. Comparing food labels can help you decide which food is more nutritious. Checking the unit price can help you figure out which product is the best deal.

MAIN IDEA AND DETAILS What are three ways that you can compare products?

What are the ingredients?

Which is the most healthful?

Which has the best price?

Lesson 4 Summary and Review

❶ Summarize with Vocabulary
Use vocabulary and other terms from this lesson to complete the statements.

Alex wants to buy the most healthful package of soup at the store. He looks at the _____ on each package. He knows that it lists the _____ in order of the amount in each package. It also has a list of _____ facts that tells about nutrients in the food.

❷ How can you find out what nutrients are in a package of food?

❸ Critical Thinking Describe two things that can affect the cost of food.

❹ (Focus Skill) COMPARE AND CONTRAST Draw and complete this graphic organizer to show how the ingredients in the canned and dried soups on page 73 are alike and how they are different.

Topic: Ingredients in canned soup and dry soup

Alike	Different

❺ Write to Inform—How-To
Explain three steps you can take to be a wise shopper.

Make Responsible Decisions

About Snacks

You make many decisions every day. Some decisions are about meals and snacks. Use the steps for **Making Responsible Decisions** to help you make healthful food choices.

Maria and her friend are going to the park. Maria wants a healthful snack for energy. What should she do?

1 Find out about the choices you could make.

Maria can eat a peach, a piece of cake, or a peanut butter sandwich.

2 Eliminate choices that are against your family's rules.

Maria knows her father would not approve of her having cake for a snack. She eliminates that choice.

3 Ask yourself: What could happen with each choice? Does the choice show good character?

4 Make what seems to be the best choice.

If Maria makes a peanut butter sandwich, her friend will have to wait for her. If she has a peach, she can eat it on the way to the park.

Maria decides to have a peach. It will give her the energy she needs, and her friend will not have to wait for her. Her decision shows that she is being responsible.

Problem Solving

Ben is bringing drinks for the baseball team. He could bring cola, fruit juice, or water.

Use the steps for **Making Responsible Decisions** to help Ben make his choice. How does Ben's choice show he is making a responsible decision?

Handling Food Safely

Lesson Focus

Foods need to be stored and handled correctly to keep them safe to eat.

Why Learn This?

You can use what you learn to help you stay well.

Vocabulary

spoiled

Preparing Food Safely

You can help prepare food safely by handling it carefully. Germs can spread easily from one food to another. Some germs can make you sick.

To keep germs from spreading, wash your hands with soap and warm water before and after handling foods. Keep your cooking tools and work areas clean.

All foods can carry germs, but raw meat and poultry are very unsafe. You should not cut other foods on a surface that has held raw meat or poultry. Wash cutting boards with soap and hot water.

CAUSE AND EFFECT **What could cause you to become sick after eating?**

◄ Wash all fruits and vegetables with plain, cold water to remove any dirt, germs, or pesticides.

Storing Food Safely

Some foods spoil. A **spoiled** food is one that is unsafe to eat. Spoiled foods might look like fresh foods, but they usually smell and taste bad. To keep foods from spoiling, you need to store them properly. Many fresh foods need to be kept in a refrigerator or freezer. Keeping foods in containers can also keep them from spoiling.

When you are putting groceries away, place frozen foods in the freezer first. They must stay frozen to be safe. Next, put meats, chicken, and eggs in the refrigerator. Then put fresh vegetables and fruits in the refrigerator.

SEQUENCE List the order in which you should put away groceries when you get home from the store.

▼ Refrigerating food at the correct temperature helps keep it safe to eat.

▼ Wrapping food or storing it in covered containers helps keep it fresh.

ACTIVITY

Building Good Character

Caring With the help of a parent or another trusted adult, prepare the family's lunch for the next day. By storing the lunches safely, you can show you care for your family's safety.

Identifying Foods for the Refrigerator List at least three things that need to be refrigerated after they are opened.

Refrigerating Food

You must refrigerate some foods to keep them safe to eat. Refrigerating foods at the proper temperature will help keep germs from multiplying quickly, and keeps foods from spoiling. The proper refrigerator temperature is 40 degrees Fahrenheit or less.

Most leftovers should be refrigerated or frozen. Opened containers of mayonnaise and canned fruit should also be refrigerated. Most foods should not be left out for more than two hours. Germs grow quickly in warm air.

DRAW CONCLUSIONS Why is it important to refrigerate foods properly?

Lesson 5 Summary and Review

1 Summarize with Vocabulary

Use vocabulary and other terms from this lesson to complete the statements.

_____ food is unsafe to eat. Meats, eggs, and milk should be placed in the _____.

2 Name three foods that must be placed in a refrigerator right away.

3 Critical Thinking Why shouldn't you eat spoiled food?

4 Focus Skill COMPARE AND CONTRAST

Draw and complete this graphic organizer.

Topic: Safe leftovers and Spoiled leftovers

Alike	Different

5 Write to Inform—Explanation

Write a pamphlet with food safety information for families. Include a list of tips for preparing, storing and handling foods safely.

ACTIVITIES

Science

Food Storage Put a slice of bread in each of two clear, zip-type bags. Seal one bag tightly. Leave the other bag unsealed. Leave the bags next to each other, on a counter. After a day, look at the slices of bread. Describe the appearance of the bread in each bag. Check both bags and describe what you see every day for a week. Explain why the two pieces of bread look similar or different.

Language Arts

Adjectives Pick one of your favorite healthful snacks. List at least five different adjectives that describe the snack you picked.

Technology Project

Use a calculator to solve these problems. The unit cost of 1 quart of orange juice is $2.50.

At the same unit cost, how much will 2 quarts of orange juice cost?

At the same unit cost, how much will $\frac{1}{2}$ quart of orange juice cost?

GO ONLINE For more activities, visit The Learning Site. www.harcourtschool.com/health

Home & Community

Communicating Discuss different new recipes with your family. Choose and prepare a new meal with your family. Write a paragraph explaining how the meal tasted.

Black Beans & Rice

Career Link

Food Inspector Suppose that you are a food inspector. Write a checklist of things you look for to make sure meats at supermarkets are safe for people to eat. List all the ways to check that meats are being handled and stored properly.

Focus Skill | Reading Skill

COMPARE AND CONTRAST

Draw and then use this graphic organizer to answer questions 1 and 2.

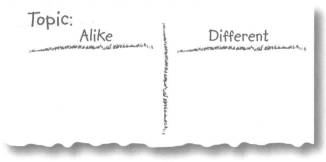

Topic:

| Alike | Different |

1 How are the wide stripes and the thin stripes from MyPyramid alike and different?

2 How are the Meats and Beans group and the Milk group alike and different?

ABC | Use Vocabulary

Match each term in Column B with its meaning in Column A.

Column A	Column B
3 Foods you eat between meals	A food guide pyramid
4 A tool to help you choose foods for a healthful diet	B spoiled
5 What you have when you eat foods from each food group every day	C snacks D balanced diet
6 A food that is unsafe to eat	E ingredients
7 Things that go into a food	

? | Check Understanding

Choose the letter of the correct answer.

8 The list of ingredients is found on _____. (p. 73)

A balanced diets   C food labels
B food groups   D unit prices

9 You should choose _____ foods from food groups with wide stripes on MyPyramid. (p. 66)

F no   H more
G fewer   I all

10 Foods originally come from plants and _____. (p. 60)

A rocks   C factories
B animals   D grocery stores

11 Healthful snacks help you get _____ you might need but not get during meals. (p. 69)

F nutrients   H oils
G fats   J sweets

12 Which of the following is **NOT** a food that needs to be refrigerated? (pp. 79–80)

A

B

C

Mixed Fruit

D

13 To compare the cost of two foods, you should look at their _____. (p. 74)

   F ingredients lists   **H** food labels

   G unit prices   **J** containers

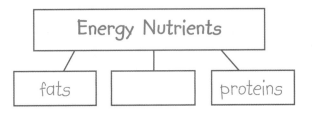

14 Which of these will complete the graphic organizer? (p. 62)

   A sugars   **C** breads

   B carbohydrates   **D** calcium

15 The ingredient found in the greatest amount will be listed _____ on a food label. (p. 73)

   F first   **H** last

   G second   **J** many times

Think Critically

16 Explain what you can do to safely handle food that has just been brought home from the grocery store.

17 Robin eats three healthful, balanced meals every day. But around 10 A.M. and 4 P.M. each day, she feels tired, weak, and hungry. Explain how Robin could change her eating habits. How will this change help her?

Apply Skills

18 **BUILDING GOOD CHARACTER**
Responsibility Hillary is bringing snacks for the art club. She could bring candy, fruit, or ice cream. What are the steps Hillary can take to make the most responsible decision?

19 **LIFE SKILLS**
Make Responsible Decisions
Suppose you are at a friend's home. You both are hungry for a snack. Your friend tells you to have a cupcake. You know a cupcake isn't a healthful snack. How can you eat a healthful snack and not hurt your friend's feelings?

Write About Health

20 **Write to Inform—Explanation** Write a paragraph explaining how understanding food labels can help you eat a healthful diet.

Activity
for a
Healthy Body

IDENTIFY CAUSE AND EFFECT An effect is something that happens. A cause is the reason the effect happens. Use the Reading in Health Handbook on pages 286–287 and this graphic organizer to help you read the health facts in this chapter.

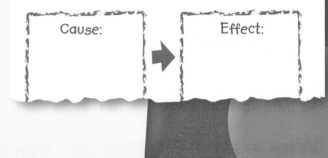

Identify Cause and Effect

| Cause: | | Effect: |

Health Graph

INTERPRET DATA Sleep is important for the health of people and other animals. Some animals need much more sleep than humans. Some animals need much less sleep than humans. How many more hours of sleep do human children need than giraffes need?

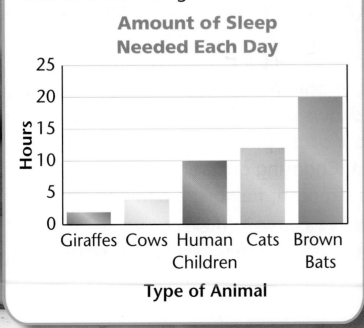

Amount of Sleep Needed Each Day

Hours

25
20
15
10
5
0

Giraffes Cows Human Children Cats Brown Bats

Type of Animal

Daily Physical Activity

Stay active for your health.

🔊 **Be Active!**
Use the selection **Track 4, Jam and Jive**, to give your heart a workout.

Keeping Your Body Fit

ACTIVITY

Life Skills

Manage Stress

If you feel stressed, exercise can help you relax. Taking a walk or riding a bike can help you feel better. Draw a picture to show some things you can do to help yourself relax when you feel stressed.

Reasons to Exercise

Exercise is any activity that makes your body work hard. Running, swimming, and jumping rope are exercises.

Exercise helps you stay fit and healthy. Exercise helps you sleep well and pay attention in school. When you get enough exercise, your body works well.

Exercise increases your strength. **Strength** is how powerful your muscles are. Exercises such as push-ups and curl-ups make your muscles strong.

Flexibility (flek•suh•BIL•uh•tee) is how easily you can move and bend. Stretching can make you more flexible.

Exercise can improve your endurance (in•DUR•ens). **Endurance** is being able to exercise for a long time without getting tired.

People of different ages need different amounts of physical activity. The Activity Pyramid shows many kinds of exercise. It shows how often people your age should do each kind. Choosing different activities increases strength, flexibility, and endurance.

IDENTIFY CAUSE AND EFFECT What is an effect of getting plenty of exercise?

The Activity Pyramid

Sitting Still
Watching television;
playing computer games
Small amounts of time

Light Exercise
Playtime, yardwork,
softball
2–3 times a week

Strength and Flexibility Exercises
Weight training, dancing,
pull-ups
2–3 times a week

Aerobic Exercises
Biking, running,
soccer, hiking
**30+ minutes, at
least 3 times a week**

Regular Activities
Walking to school; taking
the stairs; helping with
housework
Every day

Personal Health Plan ▸

Real-Life Situation
Suppose you want to get different kinds of exercise to improve your fitness.

Real-Life Plan
Write a step-by-step plan for getting the right kinds of exercise. Include the amount of time needed for each exercise.

Exercise for Fitness

Different kinds of physical activity are needed for strength, endurance, and flexibility. **Aerobic** (air•OH•bik) **exercise** causes you to breathe deeply and makes your heart beat faster. You should do an aerobic exercise for at least thirty minutes. Aerobic exercise helps your heart get stronger. It helps your lungs hold more air. It increases your endurance.

Aerobic exercises include skating, running, and biking. You should do these types of activities three times a week or more.

▼ Doing gymnastics can increase your strength and flexibility.

MAIN IDEA AND DETAILS Why should you do aerobic exercise? What two parts of your body are helped by aerobic exercise?

▲ Jumping rope is fun.
It is good exercise, too.

Exercise for Fun

Physical activities can be fun. It is a great way to spend time with your friends or family. You can also do some kinds of exercise by yourself. Many of the things you do for fun are good ways to exercise, too.

Some people play on a team. It is fun to be on a team and to learn a sport. Other people walk, ride bikes, or jump rope with friends.

People like different sports and activities. Think about what you like when you make an exercise plan. Your exercise plan should include activities that are fun. Doing things you like helps you enjoy exercising.

COMPARE AND CONTRAST Compare and contrast the physical activities you like with the physical activities a classmate likes.

Myth and Fact
Myth: Exercise makes you tired.
Fact: Exercise makes your body stronger. When you exercise, your heart pumps faster. You breathe more quickly. After you exercise, you feel more awake and alert.

▼ Exercise is fun to do with friends.

Effects of Exercise

Exercise is important for your body. It keeps your body fit and healthy.

Exercise also helps you manage stress. When you exercise, you feel good about yourself. Exercising during the day can help you sleep well at night.

Exercise is a good way to meet new people. It is fun to do with your friends and family.

MAIN IDEA AND DETAILS What are two good results of exercise?

Lesson 1 Summary and Review

① Summarize with Vocabulary
Use vocabulary terms from this lesson to complete the statements.

Any activity that makes your body work hard is _____. If you exercise, you can increase your _____, _____, and _____. You can make your heart and lungs healthier by doing _____.

② Name two physical activities you enjoy participating in.

③ Critical Thinking Why is it important to know what kinds of exercise you like?

④ (Focus Skill) IDENTIFY CAUSE AND EFFECT
Draw and complete this graphic organizer to show the effects of exercise on your body.

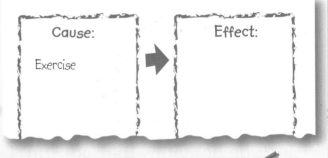

Cause:

Exercise

Effect:

⑤ Write to Inform—Explanation
Write a letter to a friend inviting her or him to join you in a physical activity at your home. Explain why the activity is fun and good for your health.

Fairness

Playing by the Rules

All sports and physical activities have rules. Rules help make games fair. When you follow the rules of a game, you are being fair to yourself and to the other players. Everyone has fun.

Following the rules can help you stay safe. Here are some simple ways to help you and others play by the rules.

- **If you don't know the rules of a game, ask a teacher or a coach.**
- **Read some books about the sport to find out the rules.**
- **Help new players learn the rules.**
- **Take some time before the game to discuss the rules. Make sure all the players understand the rules.**
- **If a player will not follow the rules, ask a teacher or a coach for help.**
- **Be a good example. Always follow the rules and be a good sport.**

Activity

Suppose someone doesn't follow the rules when you are playing a sport. With a classmate, write and perform a skit that shows how you would ask a teacher or coach for help to solve the problem.

Building Good Character

Staying Safe While Exercising

Lesson Focus

Exercising safely means following some simple safety rules.

Why Learn This?

Most injuries can be prevented. If you are injured, you should know what to do.

Vocabulary

safety gear
warm-up
cool-down
mouth guard

Exercise Safely

Following safety rules helps you stay safe when you exercise. For some exercises and most sports, you must wear safety gear. **Safety gear** is clothing or equipment that helps protect you. You should also drink plenty of water when you exercise.

Warm-Up A **warm-up** is a way to get your body ready for exercise. A warm-up can help you avoid injury when you exercise. For a good warm-up, do a gentle exercise such as jogging in place. Then lightly stretch your muscles for fifteen to twenty seconds. Repeat the stretches at least three times.

Quick Activity

Plan an Exercise Routine Write a plan for a good exercise routine. List what you would expect at the end of each week and the end of each month.

Sit-and-Reach Stretch Remember to bend at the waist. Keep your eyes on your toes. Don't lock your knees.

Calf Stretch Keep both feet flat on the floor during this exercise.

Workout After you have warmed up, you are ready to exercise. Take a minute to think about safety rules. For some kinds of exercise, like bike riding, you need a helmet. Make sure you use the safety gear you need.

During your workout, your body loses water. Most of the water is lost as sweat. If your body loses too much water, you can get sick. You need to drink water before, during, and after exercise.

Cool-Down After your workout, you should do some slow exercises. You should also do some stretches. This is called a **cool-down**. During the cool-down, your heart rate slows. A five-minute cool-down helps keep your muscles from getting sore.

SEQUENCE List the three steps for exercising safely.

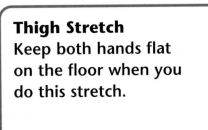

Running
You should warm up before and cool down after you run. Wear proper shoes.

Shoulder-and Chest Stretch
Pull your hands slowly toward the floor. Keep your elbows straight but not locked.

Thigh Stretch
Keep both hands flat on the floor when you do this stretch.

Play Safely

For many sports, you need to wear safety gear. One kind of safety gear is a mouth guard. A **mouth guard** is a plastic shield. Mouth guards help protect your teeth. They also protect your gums and your jaw.

For some sports, you must wear a helmet. These sports include hockey and football. You also need to wear a helmet to be safe when you bike or skate. You should wear wrist guards, elbow pads, and kneepads when you skate. They help protect you if you fall.

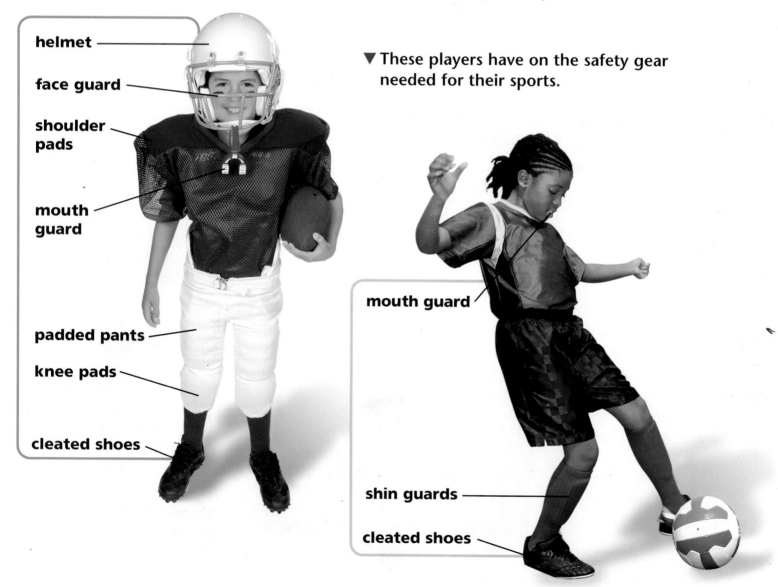

▼ These players have on the safety gear needed for their sports.

helmet

face guard

shoulder pads

mouth guard

padded pants

knee pads

cleated shoes

mouth guard

shin guards

cleated shoes

You can have fun in or around the water if you follow safety rules. ▶

Swimming is great exercise. It is a good activity to do with friends. Swimming can increase your flexibility and endurance. But water can also be dangerous if you don't follow these safety rules:

- Learn to swim.
- Never swim alone.
- Always have an adult watching you.
- Never swim during a storm.
- Wear a life jacket if you can't swim.
- Don't use pool toys to help you swim.
- Follow the lifeguard's instructions.

For more information about safety around water, see pages 304–305.

SUMMARIZE What rules help you stay safe when you swim or play near water?

Health & Technology

High-Tech Lifeguards
Lifeguards are trained to keep swimmers safe. Lifeguards must be excellent swimmers and know first aid. At some pools, technology helps lifeguards. One system uses sound waves to find swimmers who are at the bottom of the pool. An alarm tells the lifeguards a swimmer is in trouble. Another system uses cameras and computers to see underwater. Technology can help lifeguards keep swimmers safe.

If you feel pain when you are exercising, you should stop right away. Tell your parents, your coach, or your teacher.

Sprains and strains can be treated with rest and ice. Rest will keep the injury from getting worse. Ice can help keep the injured area from swelling. A bandage also can be used to reduce swelling. You should keep an injured arm or leg lifted. You can use a footstool or pillows to lift an injured arm or leg.

▼ Wrap ice in a towel or cloth before you put it on your injury.

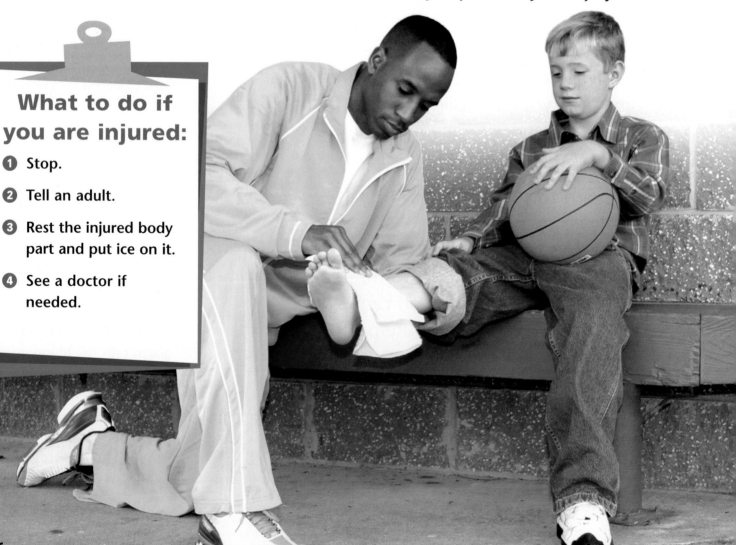

What to do if you are injured:

❶ Stop.

❷ Tell an adult.

❸ Rest the injured body part and put ice on it.

❹ See a doctor if needed.

Some injuries should be checked by a doctor. The doctor may bandage your injury. You may need medicine. If you have a broken bone, the doctor may put a cast on it. He or she will tell you how to take care of it.

If you have a serious injury, your doctor may send you to a physical therapist. Therapists use physical exercises to help injuries heal.

SEQUENCE What are the first two things you should do if you are injured while exercising?

Lesson 2 Summary and Review

1 Summarize with Vocabulary

Use vocabulary terms from this lesson to complete the statements.

Before you exercise, a _____ can help your body get ready. After you exercise, you should do a _____. Clothing and equipment needed to prevent injury in sports are called _____. A _____ will help keep your teeth, your gums, and your jaw safe.

2 What are some ways to stay safe in or near water?

3 Critical Thinking Why should you stop right away if you feel pain when you are exercising?

4 (Focus Skill) **IDENTIFY CAUSE AND EFFECT**

Draw and complete this graphic organizer to show the effects of following safety rules.

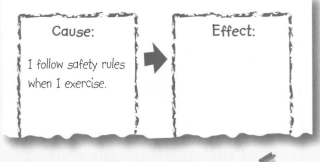

Cause:

I follow safety rules when I exercise.

Effect:

5 Write to Inform—Explanation

Write a paragraph explaining the safety rules for playing a sport you like.

Make Responsible Decisions
With Safety in Mind

The decisions you make can help keep you safe. They can help you avoid injuries. Using the steps for **Making Responsible Decisions** can help you make safe choices.

Harrison meets his friends to play soccer. He sees that he has forgotten his shin guards. What should Harrison do?

1 **Find out about the choices you could make.**

2 **Say *no* to choices that are against your family rules.**

Harrison has three choices. He could play without his shin guards, sit and watch his friends play, or he could go home to get his shin guards.

Harrison knows his parents would not want him to play soccer without his shin guards.

3 Ask yourself: What could happen with each choice? Does the choice show good character?

4 Make what seems to be the best choice.

If Harrison doesn't play, his team will not have enough players.

Harrison goes home to get his shin guards before he plays.

Problem Solving

Marisa is walking alone near a pond on a hot day. Marisa knows that people sometimes swim in the pond. Right now, Marisa's parents are not nearby. Marisa would like to take a quick swim in the pond.

How could Marisa use the steps for **Making Responsible Decisions** to make the best decision? How would Marisa's decision show she is responsible?

Chapter Review and Test Preparation

Reading Skill

IDENTIFY CAUSE AND EFFECT

Draw and then use this graphic organizer to answer questions 1 and 2.

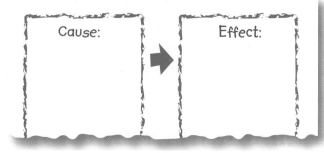

Cause: → Effect:

1 Write at least two effects of this cause: *I follow safety rules when I play sports.*

2 Write at least two effects of this cause: *I set a goal to get enough sleep.*

Use Vocabulary

Match each term in Column B with its meaning in Column A.

Column A	Column B
3 How well your muscles and joints move and bend	**A** endurance
4 Any activity that makes your body work hard	**B** strength
	C warm-up
5 Slow stretches after exercise	**D** flexibility
	E cool-down
6 How powerful your muscles are	**F** exercise
7 A way to get your body ready for exercise	
8 The ability to exercise for a long time without getting tired	

Check Understanding

Choose the letter of the correct answer.

9 How much sleep should you try to get each night? (p. 101)
A less than two hours
B more than sixteen hours
C exactly eight hours
D at least ten hours

10 To protect your teeth and gums during sports, you can use a _____. (p. 94)
F shin guard
G mouth guard
H shoulder pad
J warm-up

11 Aerobic exercise increases your _____. (p. 88)
A cool-down
B endurance
C stress
D safety gear

12 If you are planning a bike ride, which of the following must you use? (p. 94)

F

H

G

J

Cause		Effect
I get enough rest.	→	

13 Which of the following effects would best complete the graphic organizer? (p. 100)

A I feel tired.

B I'm in a bad mood.

C I can't think well.

D I feel good.

14 What does a warm-up do? (p. 92)

F gets your body ready for exercise

G gives a good aerobic workout

H increases your chance of getting hurt

J helps you cool down after exercise

15 Mouth guards are most useful for preventing _____. (p. 94)

A broken teeth

B shin injuries

C broken wrists

D head injuries

Think Critically

16 You enjoy playing with other students. You also enjoy running and jumping. You need to make a physical fitness plan. What sport might you want to include in your fitness plan? Explain why you chose this activity.

17 You have set a goal to get more aerobic exercise. Your friend wants you to watch television with her instead. What are two things you could tell your friend?

Apply Skills

18 BUILDING GOOD CHARACTER
Fairness You have been invited to play baseball with your cousin's family. After the game has started, you notice that your cousin's family uses some rules that are new to you. Apply what you know about fairness to decide what to do.

19 LIFE SKILLS
Make Responsible Decisions
You are invited to swim at a friend's house. You notice that there are no adults watching the pool. Apply what you know about making decisions with safety in mind to decide what to do.

Write About Health

20 **Write to Inform—Explanation**
Explain how a healthful amount of exercise now can help you become a healthy adult.

Keeping Safe

Focus Skill

Reading Skill

DRAW CONCLUSIONS You use information from your reading plus what you already know to draw a conclusion. Use the Reading in Health Handbook on pages 284–285 and this graphic organizer to help you read the health facts in this chapter.

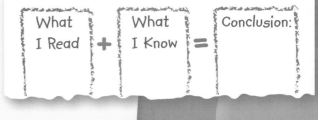

Draw Conclusions

What I Read	+	What I Know	=	Conclusion:

Health Graph

INTERPRET DATA Every year thousands of children are injured in accidents involving cars and bicycles. How many more children were injured in car crashes than in pedestrian accidents? How many more were injured in bicycle accidents than in car accidents?

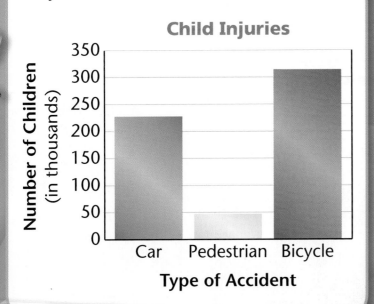

Child Injuries

Number of Children (in thousands)

350
300
250
200
150
100
50
0

Car   Pedestrian   Bicycle

Type of Accident

Daily Physical Activity

Physical activities can be fun. Remember to stay safe.

🎵 *Be Active!*
Use the selection **Track 5**, **Flexercise**, to practice safe warm-ups and exercises.

Being Responsible for Your Safety

Lesson Focus
You can help keep yourself and others safe by following safety rules.

Why Learn This?
What you learn about safety can help you protect yourself and others from harm.

Vocabulary
limit
safety rules
injury
hazard
passenger

Be Responsible and Careful

Many people help keep you safe. Family members have a responsibility to protect you from harm. Your family sets limits. A **limit** is a point that you may not go beyond. The time you must be home from playing is a limit.

To be safe, you must be careful. This means that you know and follow safety rules. **Safety rules** are rules that help protect you from an injury. An **injury** (IN•juh•ree) is harm done to a person's body.

You can also be safe by watching out for hazards. A **hazard** (HAZ•uhrd) is a danger that could lead to an injury.

Focus Skill **DRAW CONCLUSIONS Why does your family set limits for you?**

Quick Activity

Identify Helpers
Make a list of people who help keep you safe. List everyone you can think of.

Family

Teacher

Crossing Guard

Be Safe on the Road

When you ride in a car or bus with a driver, you are a **passenger** (PAS·en·jer). There are rules for passengers as well as for drivers. Rules for riding in a car or bus and rules for walking are on this page.

SUMMARIZE How can you stay safe when you are a passenger in a car?

ACTIVITY

Building Good Character

Citizenship When Tony walks to school, he walks on the sidewalk and crosses the street only at corners. How does this show that Tony cares about his community?

Walking
- Stay on the sidewalk.
- Walk with others, not alone.
- Cross streets only at corners or crosswalks. Before crossing, STOP, LOOK, and LISTEN. THINK about what might be a hazard.

Riding in a Bus
- Do not bother the bus driver.
- Stay in your seat.
- Talk quietly. Never yell.

Riding in a Car
- Always stay in your seat with your safety belt buckled.
- Sit in the back seat.
- If you are less than 57 inches tall, use a booster seat.
- Do not lean on or put your hands out the window.

Be Safe at School

Obeying safety rules at school and places where people work helps keep you and others from getting hurt. Some rules at your school include not running in the halls or stairways. Be sure to follow game rules on the playground. Don't push or shove.

Another way to be safe is to get help from an adult. If you see a fight, tell an adult. If you see a weapon, such as a gun or a knife, don't touch it. Tell an adult right away.

SUMMARIZE Why should you obey safety rules while at school and work places?

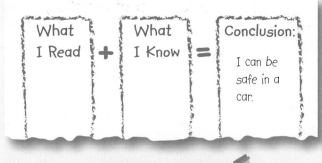

Lesson 1 Summary and Review

❶ Summarize with Vocabulary
Use vocabulary from this lesson to complete the statements.

When you follow _____, you are being careful. An _____ is harm done to the body. A danger that could lead to an injury is called a _____. Adults set _____ to help keep you safe. Follow safety rules when you are a _____ in a car.

❷ List three ways to avoid being injured while walking to school.

❸ Critical Thinking Why is it important to take responsibility for your own safety?

❹ (Focus Skill) DRAW CONCLUSIONS Draw and complete this graphic organizer to show safety rules to follow when riding in a car.

| What I Read | + | What I Know | = | Conclusion: I can be safe in a car. |

❺ Write to Inform—How-To
Write a newspaper article about how to stay safe at school. Include a list of safety rules that students can follow.

110

Responsibility

Your Own Safety at School

Many people take care of you at school—your teachers, the principal, the school nurse, and others. They help make sure you are safe. Another person also has the responsibililty to keep you safe. That person is YOU. Here are some ways for taking responsibility for your own safety.

- **Know what to do if there is an emergency.**
- **Don't run in hallways or stairways.**
- **Don't push, shove, or fight with other students.**
- **Follow playground rules and use playground equipment properly.**
- **Avoid bullies. Tell a trusted adult if someone threatens you.**
- **Know where school safety equipment is stored.**
- **Wear proper safety equipment when playing sports or working in a science lab.**

Activity

With a group of students, write a skit about safety rules. Perform your skit for the rest of the class, and ask classmates to identify the safe behaviors you act out.

Safety Around Others

Lesson Focus

You can follow safety rules to protect yourself from strangers and bullies.

Why Learn This?

You can use what you learn to help yourself stay safe around strangers and bullies.

Vocabulary

stranger
bully
trusted adult

Strangers and Bullies

A **stranger** is someone you don't know well. Some strangers aren't safe to be around. For this reason, you should follow safety rules if a stranger causes you to be afraid.

Never take anything, such as candy, money, or toys, from a stranger. If a stranger asks you for help, such as to find a lost pet, tell him or her *NO*. Then leave the area and find help. Always stay more than an arm's reach away from a stranger.

Quick Activity

Analyze Safety Rules
List the safety rules about strangers. Add at least two other rules to the list.

If a stranger in a car stops and calls to you, ignore him or her. Keep walking, cross the street, or change direction. Never go anywhere with a stranger. If a stranger tries to come after you, run away and yell "I don't know you!"

Another way to protect yourself from strangers is to *always* tell your family where you are going and whom you will be with.

A **bully** is someone who hurts or frightens others. Read the following story from Jake's journal.

▲ Choosing friends wisely can help you avoid being friends with a bully. Bullies should be left alone.

One day after school, a boy in my class started following me and calling me names. Then he pushed me against a wall. I got away. My friends saw what happened. We told our teacher. That night I didn't sleep well.

The next day, our class talked about bullies. We learned that we shouldn't listen to mean things a bully says. We also learned that we should just walk away from a bully. Name-calling and hitting are not ways to deal with bullies.

IDENTIFY MAIN IDEA AND DETAILS
What is the main idea of Jake's journal entry?

ACTIVITY

Life Skills
Communicate
Lauren teases Helen because she has freckles and red hair. Helen feels sad when someone teases her. Tell ways Helen can communicate how she feels about being teased.

Personal Health Plan ▶

Real-Life Situation
Preventing dangerous situations is one way to keep yourself safe.

Real-Life Plan
Make a list of things you can do to keep safe from violence, gangs, and weapons.

Avoid Violence

Violence (VY•uh•luhns) is anything that someone does that harms another person. Violence includes fighting or saying you will hurt another person.

You can avoid violence by not fighting. If someone is teasing you or pushing you, walk away. Learn how to solve conflicts by talking and compromising. Make friends with people who do not do harmful things to others and are not in a gang. If you are afraid to go to school because someone is violent, tell your parents or your teacher.

DRAW CONCLUSIONS **Explain why you should avoid violence, gangs, and weapons.**

▼ If you see a weapon, such as a gun or knife, don't touch it. Instead, tell an adult right away.

How to Get Help

If you need help, find a trusted adult. A **trusted adult** is a grown-up you know well or an adult in a responsible position. Parents or other family members, teachers, good neighbors, security people, and police officers are adults you usually can trust.

If you are lost or being followed, dial 911 at a pay phone. It's a free call. Also, you can go into a store and ask someone who works there for help.

MAIN IDEA AND DETAILS Where can you get help if you are lost?

▲ If you get separated from your parents while out shopping, ask a trusted adult for help.

Lesson 2 Summary and Review

❶ Summarize with Vocabulary

Use vocabulary and other terms from this lesson to complete the statements.

Someone that you do not know well is a _____. Someone who hurts or frightens others is a _____. If someone is bothering you, look for a _____ adult. _____ is something that someone does that hurts another person.

❷ Critical Thinking Why is bullying harmful?

❸ List five people you know who are trusted adults.

❹ (Focus Skill) DRAW CONCLUSIONS Draw and complete this graphic organizer about ways to avoid violence.

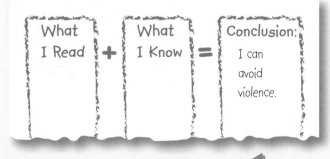

❺ Write to Inform—Narration

Choose the safety rule from this lesson that you think is the most important. Write a paragraph that explains why you think so.

Resolve Conflicts
Using Negotiation

Disagreements happen, even among friends. Knowing ways to work things out will help you get along better.

Ramon, Leah, and John want to play table tennis. They argue about who gets to play first. How can they use the steps for **Resolving Conflicts** to solve their problem?

1 **Use "I" messages to tell how you feel.**

2 **Listen to each other. Consider the other person's view.**

Leah tells her friends that she would like to play first. She explains that she did not get to play at all the last time everyone played.

Ramon explains that he has to go home soon. John says that he won the last time and should be first this time.

③ Negotiate.

Ramon, Leah, and John consider how to be fair about deciding who gets to play first. Each makes a suggestion about how to solve the problem.

④ Compromise on a solution.

John, Ramon, and Leah decide that all three can play together until Ramon has to leave. Then Leah and John will play against each other.

Problem Solving

Kim visited at Erin's home after school. Kim wanted to play outside, but Erin wanted to play computer games.

Use the steps for **Resolving Conflicts** to show how they could solve this problem. How can their decision show fairness?

Safety on Wheels

Lesson Focus
Wear proper safety gear to help prevent injuries.

Why Learn This?
Learning how to stay safe while playing can help you avoid injuries.

Consumer Activity

Access Valid Health Information Using the Internet or research books, make a picture time line of the safety features of bicycles.

Sports on Wheels

People who play sports on wheels often get injured. When bicycling, skateboarding, skating, and riding scooters, be sure to wear special safety gear. Using the right gear can help keep you from getting hurt.

Safety Equipment for Sports on Wheels

Sport	Equipment
Bicycling	Bicycle helmet
Skateboarding	Skating helmet, knee pads, elbow pads, wrist guards
Skating	Skating helmet, knee pads, elbow pads, wrist guards
Scooters	Skating helmet, knee pads, elbow pads

Safety gear isn't the only thing that can keep you safe when riding a bike. Follow these rules. Carry only one person—you. If you have to carry a backpack for school, place it in a basket. Walk your bike across streets. Ride only in daylight. If you ride when it's cloudy or rainy, wear reflective clothing.

 DRAW CONCLUSIONS **Why is it important to wear safety gear when playing sports on wheels?**

Buying a Helmet

When buying a helmet, think about these things. Make sure the helmet fits. To test the fit, try it on. Fit all the pads and adjust the straps. The helmet should fit level on your head and low on your forehead. Try to pull the helmet off. If it comes off, adjust the straps. Then try again. If it comes off again, try another helmet. Choose a bright color that others can see.

COMPARE AND CONTRAST How are the safety equipment needed for bicycling and the equipment for skating alike? How are they different?

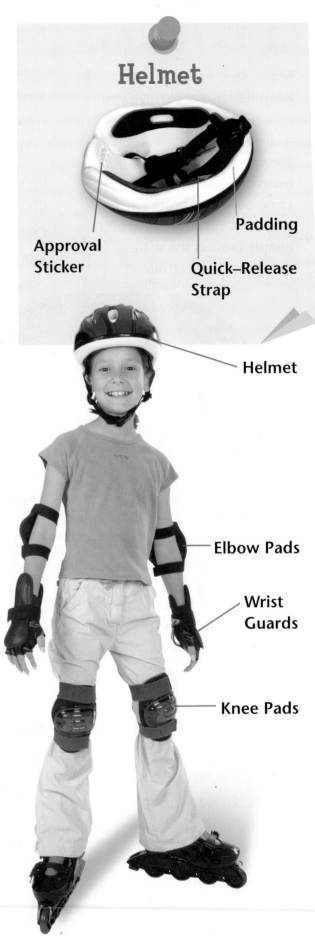

Helmet

Approval Sticker

Padding

Quick–Release Strap

Helmet

Elbow Pads

Wrist Guards

Knee Pads

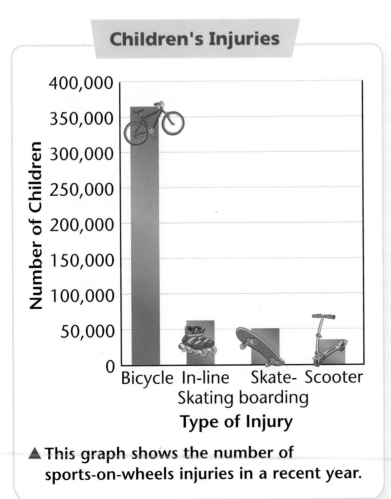

Children's Injuries

▲ This graph shows the number of sports-on-wheels injuries in a recent year.

Move Out of My Way!

Beep! Beep! Beep! Have you ever heard that sound when a large truck is backing up? Some cars, trucks, and minivans now make the same beeping sound when they back up. The noise tells people behind the vehicle that they'd better move!

Safety Around Vehicles

Today, cars and trucks are everywhere. Knowing how to be safe around vehicles is important so you won't be hit by them.

Here's what you should know. Don't play in driveways, streets, or parking lots. Always cross the street at a corner with a light or a crossing guard. Look before running into the street after a ball or a pet. Watch for cars that are turning or backing up.

Focus Skill **DRAW CONCLUSIONS Why should you be careful around driveways and parking lots?**

Beep...Beep...Beep...

Lesson 3 Summary and Review

1 Summarize with Vocabulary
Use terms from this lesson to complete the statements.

When playing sports on wheels, you should always wear proper _____. It will protect you from an _____. A _____ can protect your head. You can protect your knees and elbows by wearing _____.

2 Critical Thinking Why is it important for a bicycle helmet to fit properly?

3 List three safety rules to follow when you are around vehicles.

4 Focus Skill DRAW CONCLUSIONS Draw and complete this graphic organizer to show safety rules for bicycling.

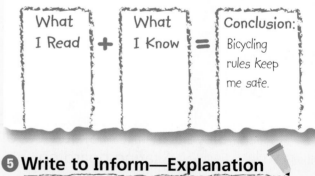

| What I Read | + | What I Know | = | Conclusion: Bicycling rules keep me safe. |

5 Write to Inform—Explanation
Write a paragraph that explains why wearing a helmet while playing sports on wheels is important.

ACTIVITIES

Physical Education

Protecting Bones Find a diagram of the skeletal system in this book or a reference source. Point out and name the bones that are protected by the safety gear mentioned in this chapter.

Science

Inventions That Save Lives
Investigate inventions that have helped make cars safer for drivers and passengers. Make a time line to show the sequence of the development of these safety features.

Technology Project

Use a camera to take a picture of someone in the correct safety gear for bicycling. Use a computer to make a label for each piece of safety gear. Attach the labels to the picture in the correct spots. Use pp. 118–119 if you need help.

GO ONLINE For more activities, visit The Learning Site.
www.harcourtschool.com/health

Home & Community

Communicating With your family, find out how your community playground can be made into a safer place to play. Then write a letter to a local official, explaining what improvements could be made.

Career Link

Security Guard Security guards work to make sure people are safe in places where they work, play, and shop. They also answer questions and help people who are lost or in trouble. Suppose you were a security guard at an amusement park. How would you help keep people safe? Write a list of things you would do.

Reading Skill

Focus Skill

SEQUENCE To sequence is to place events in the order in which they happen. It can also be to list in order the steps for carrying out a task. Use the Reading in Health Handbook on pages 290–291 and this graphic organizer to help you read the health facts in this chapter.

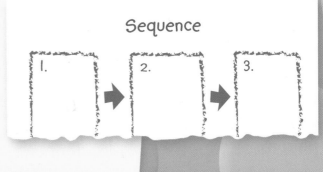

Sequence

1. 2. 3.

Health Graph

INTERPRET DATA Earthquakes are described by their strength. The strongest earthquakes are described as major. About how many earthquakes happen each year? About how many are major earthquakes?

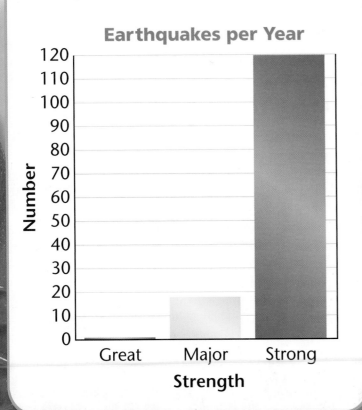

Earthquakes per Year

Number

120
110
100
90
80
70
60
50
40
30
20
10
0

Great   Major   Strong

Strength

Daily Physical Activity

Be active and stay safe inside and outside your home.

Be Active!
Use the selection **Track 6**, **Muscle Mambo**, to move your heart and other muscles toward good health.

Safety Around Fire and Poisons

Lesson Focus

You and your family can take steps to protect yourselves from fire and poisons.

Why Learn This?

What you learn can help keep you and your family safe from fires and poisons.

Vocabulary

emergency
poison

Emergency

What's that beeping noise? It sounds like the smoke alarm. You smell smoke. Someone yells, "Fire!" You know there is a fire in your house. This is an emergency (ih•MER•juhnt•see). An **emergency** is a situation in which help is needed right away. Everyone should know what to do in an emergency.

First you and your family can work together to make an escape plan. Then you can practice fire drills. Decide on a place outdoors to meet after you escape.

 **SEQUENCE What should you do before you practice fire drills at home?**

Quick Activity

Make an Escape Map
Draw a map of your home. Use arrows to show at least two ways you would get out if a fire happened.

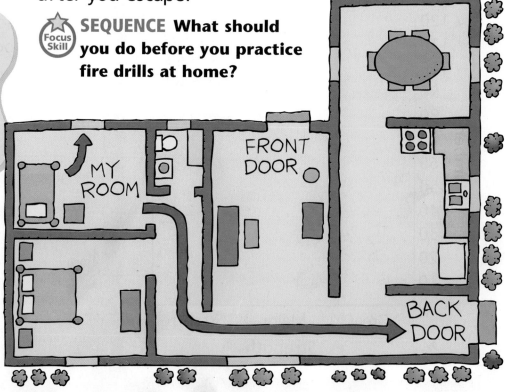

MY ROOM

FRONT DOOR

BACK DOOR

Escaping from Fire

Here's how to escape from a fire.

Crawl Out Quickly.
Drop down and stay below the smoke. If possible, hold a damp cloth over your mouth and nose so you don't breathe the smoke.

Warn Others.
Shout or blow a whistle loudly to warn your family.

Go to the Meeting Place.
Make sure you go to the meeting place so your family doesn't think you are trapped inside the house.

Call 911.
Tell the 911 operator your address. The operator may also ask other questions. Don't hang up before you are told to.

Stop, Drop, and Roll.
If your clothing catches fire, stop and drop to the ground. Roll slowly back and forth to put out the fire.

Stop   Drop   Roll

SEQUENCE **What should you do if your clothing catches fire?**

Focus Skill

Safety Around Poisons

A **poison** (POY•zuhn) is a substance that causes illness, injury, or death when it gets on the skin or into the body. Many useful home products are poisons if they aren't used the right way. Many products are harmful if they are breathed in, swallowed, or touched. Even medicines can be harmful if they aren't used the right way. Arts and crafts materials with strong odors can be poisons, too. Don't use them unless you have windows open and fresh air coming in. Don't breathe the odors.

Cleaning products should be locked up where small children can't reach them. If you see a poison where a young child might touch it, tell a parent or another trusted adult right away.

CAUSE AND EFFECT What might happen if a person breathes in a poison?

Personal Health Plan ▸

Real-Life Situation
Most product labels tell the right way to use the product. The label also tells the dangers of using the product the wrong way.

Real-Life Plan
Make a list of ways you might use product labels to keep safe from poisons.

Lesson 1 Summary and Review

❶ Summarize with Vocabulary
Use vocabulary and other terms from this lesson to complete the statements.

A house fire is an _____. You can know what to do in an emergency by making a family _____. If your clothing catches fire, stop, drop, and _____. A _____ is a substance that causes illness or death when it gets on or into the body.

❷ Critical Thinking Why should you give the 911 operator your address?

❸ How can you keep young children safe around cleaning products?

❹ (Focus Skill) **SEQUENCE** Draw and complete this graphic organizer to show the steps to follow in case of fire.

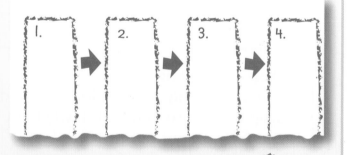

❺ Write to Inform—Narration
Write a short story about a family who escapes from a fire.

Citizenship

Obeying Rules and Laws for Safety

Rules and laws are made to protect everyone. By obeying safety rules and laws, you show respect for yourself and others. You help everyone around you live in a safe place. Here are some rules and laws that help you stay safe.

- **Obey signs that warn of danger.**
- **Obey signs that tell you to stay out of a certain place.**
- **Cross streets only at corners. Cross when the light is green or when you have a walk signal.**
- **When walking to or from school, stay on streets where there are other people. Don't take shortcuts through alleys or vacant lots.**
- **When riding on a school bus, find a seat and sit down. Obey the bus driver.**
- **Don't ride your bike in areas that are marked only for cars or only for people walking.**
- **Don't swim alone or where swimming is unsafe or not allowed.**

Activity

Obeying classroom rules is another way to be a good citizen. Make a list of classroom rules. Place a check mark after each rule every time you follow it. Keep track for one week. How can you get more checks the next week?

129

Home Safety

Electricity

Electricity (ih•lek•TRIS•uh•tee) is a form of energy that can produce light, heat, and motion. Without electricity, you wouldn't have TVs or microwave ovens. But electricity can also be harmful. If not used the right way, it can cause fires and electric shocks.

Electrical cords carry electricity throughout your home. They are safe to use, but only when they aren't cracked or worn out. Read the other rules on the chart below for using electricity safely.

CAUSE AND EFFECT What might happen if you use electrical cords that are worn out?

Lesson Focus
Following safety rules at home can protect you and your family.

Why Learn This?
What you learn can help keep you and your family safe at home.

Vocabulary
electricity

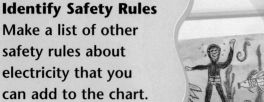

Quick Activity

Identify Safety Rules
Make a list of other safety rules about electricity that you can add to the chart.

Safety Around Electricity

- When unplugging things, hold the plug, not the cord.
- Use only one plug in each outlet.
- Never run cords under a carpet.
- Don't plug in or turn on electrical things when your hands are wet.
- Never touch outdoor power lines.

ACTIVITY

Building Good Character

Responsibility You are at a friend's house after school. She wants to use the stove to make a snack. She tells you that her mother said she can use the stove any time she wants. How can you show responsible behavior?

▲ Be careful when removing food from a microwave. Steam can escape and burn you, even if the container isn't hot. Never use a microwave if its door doesn't close tightly.

Kitchen Safety

Do you ever prepare a meal or a snack for yourself? You should follow kitchen safety rules to avoid burns, cuts, and other injuries.

Always ask a parent or another trusted adult before you use any kitchen appliances. Be sure the countertops are dry before plugging in a toaster or other electrical appliance. Use only butter knives, never sharp ones. When carrying scissors, be sure the blades are pointing down. If you break a glass, ask an adult to help clean up the broken glass.

MAIN IDEA AND DETAILS Tell three ways you can practice kitchen safety.

Did You Know?

Kitchen Fires Many fires can be put out with water. But don't throw water on a grease fire. The water will only spread the fire. Use a fire extinguisher or baking soda to put out a grease fire.

ACTIVITY

Life Skills

Make Responsible Decisions

You and a friend are skating in the park. Your friend falls. Her knees are scraped and bleeding. She can't stand on one of her injured legs. What should you do?

Be sure your first-aid kit includes these things: emergency phone numbers, clean bandages, tape, sharp scissors, tweezers, rubber gloves, and medicine to treat an allergic reaction.

First Aid

Have you ever been injured or seen someone injured? Did you know what to do? For a serious injury, the most important thing you can do is get help. At school, tell a teacher. At home, tell a family member or another adult. If you can't find an adult, call 911.

You can treat minor injuries with simple first aid. For a cut or scrape, wash the injury with clean drinking water. Don't put soap on the injury. Next, clean the area around the injury with mild soap and a washcloth. Then, cover the injury with a clean bandage. Tell a parent or another adult about the cut as soon as possible. Never touch another person's blood or anything with blood on it. If a person is bleeding, get help.

You can also treat insect stings with simple first aid. Scrape out—don't pull—the stinger. Wash the injury. Put ice or a cold pack on it for a few minutes. If you have trouble breathing, feel sick to your stomach, or get dizzy, tell an adult or call 911 immediately.

Choking is an emergency that also needs immediate attention. If you're choking near other people, make the universal choking sign. If you're alone, place your fist above your navel. Grab your fist with your other hand. Then pull your hands in and up with a quick, hard thrust. If this doesn't work and it's hard to breathe, get help!

▲ The universal choking sign—grasping the throat with both hands—means that a person is choking and needs help.

SUMMARIZE **Tell how to treat an insect sting.**

Lesson 2 Summary and Review

❶ Summarize with Vocabulary

Use vocabulary and other terms from this lesson to complete the statements.

A form of energy that can produce light, heat, and motion is _____. You can treat minor injuries with simple _____. If you get a _____ or scrape, you should wash it with clean drinking water.

❷ Critical Thinking What safety rules should you follow when you plug in a lamp?

❸ What should you do if someone is badly injured?

❹ (Focus Skill) SEQUENCE Draw and complete this graphic organizer to show the first-aid steps to follow when treating a cut or scrape.

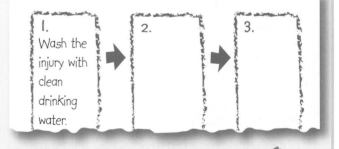

❺ Write to Inform—Explanation

Write a radio announcement. Inform listeners why knowing kitchen safety rules is important.

Communicate with Others

About Emergencies

How can you get help in an emergency? You may have to communicate with others. Using the steps for **Communicating** can help you get the help you need.

Cassie is outside her house. She sees smoke coming from the house down the street. What should she do?

 Decide who you should talk with.

Cassie sees smoke. She knows it is an emergency. Cassie knows she must call 911 for help.

2 **Give a clear message. Express ideas in a clear, organized way.**

Cassie tells the 911 operator that there is a fire emergency. She clearly tells her name and where she is calling from.

3 **Listen carefully, and answer any questions.**

4 **Gather feedback.**

What's the address?

The address is. . .

Cassie stays calm and speaks slowly. She answers the operator's questions as best she can.

Cassie sees the fire truck. But she stays on the phone. She knows she shouldn't hang up until she's told to.

Problem Solving

After school, Juan and some friends are playing on school grounds. One of the boys falls and cuts his mouth. He is bleeding. The school is locked, but there is a house next door to the school. Juan knows that his friend needs help. Use the steps for **Communicating** to show how Juan should act.

Describe how Juan's actions could show that he is caring and responsible.

LESSON 3

Disaster Safety

Types of Disasters

A **disaster** (dih•ZAS•ter) is an event that causes widespread damage. Some disasters are caused by weather. These natural disasters happen every year all over the world. Some natural disasters may happen where you live.

One type of natural disaster is an *earthquake*. An earthquake happens when the ground shakes, slides, or rolls. An earthquake can be mild or forceful.

A *tornado* is a very strong windstorm. The winds spin in a cloud that is shaped like a funnel. A tornado can destroy homes and other buildings.

Lesson Focus
Planning ahead helps prevent injuries from a disaster.

Why Learn This?
What you learn can help keep you and your family safe in disasters.

Vocabulary
disaster

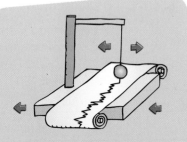

Myth and Fact
Myth: Scientists can predict when and where an earthquake will happen.
Fact: No scientist has ever been able to predict a major earthquake.

▼ Which of these five disasters happen near where you live?

136

A *hurricane* is a violent storm with strong winds and heavy rain. Hurricanes form over water. Flooding from a hurricane can cause much damage.

An *electrical storm* is a storm with strong winds, heavy rain, and lightning. Lightning is dangerous if it hits you. A *blizzard* is a dangerous snowstorm. It has strong winds and a lot of snowfall.

Some disasters are not natural. Instead, they are caused by people. For example, some groups of people do violent things to get what they want. These acts are called *terrorism*. Being well prepared for any disaster can help prevent injury or even save your life.

COMPARE AND CONTRAST How are a blizzard and an electrical storm alike and different?

Consumer Activity

Access Valid Health Information Visit or write your local health department, city hall, or library. Ask for information on how to prepare for disasters in your area. Share your findings with the class.

NOAA Weather Radio is a group of radio stations. They broadcast twenty-four hours a day. The stations give warnings, watches, forecasts, and other important information about weather hazards. They also report chemical or oil spills.

Plan for Emergencies

You can't do anything to stop disasters. But you can plan for them. Planning helps prevent injuries.

Know where to go if you must leave your home because of a disaster. Know how to get there. If you live in an area that has blizzards or hurricanes, keep supply kits in the house. They should include food, water, a flashlight, blankets, extra batteries, and a first-aid kit. Keep a radio that runs on batteries in your home. Radio reports give warnings about disasters. They also tell you what to do during disasters.

At school, listen carefully during disaster drills. Then you'll know what to do at school during a disaster.

SUMMARIZE List three ways you can plan for emergencies.

Quick Activity

Make a List Look at the items in the pantry. Make a list of items you would need to keep on hand in the case of a disaster.

What to Do in an Emergency

During any emergency, you should do what your parent, teacher, or other trusted adult tells you to do. Also, follow the tips below.

Tornado Go to a basement. Stay away from windows. If you do not have a basement, go into a closet or a hall without windows or crawl into a bathtub. Putting a mattress over you will help keep falling objects from injuring you.

Earthquake During an earthquake, crawl under a heavy desk or stand in a doorway. If possible, go outside and stay away from walls of buildings.

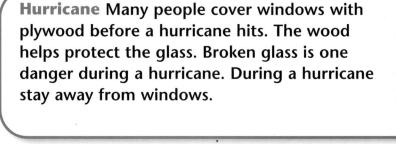

Hurricane Many people cover windows with plywood before a hurricane hits. The wood helps protect the glass. Broken glass is one danger during a hurricane. During a hurricane stay away from windows.

Electrical Storm During an electrical storm, don't use a telephone or run water. Lightning can enter a house through telephone wires or water pipes. If you're outdoors, don't stand under a tree. Trees often get struck by lightning. Crouch on the ground, away from tall objects.

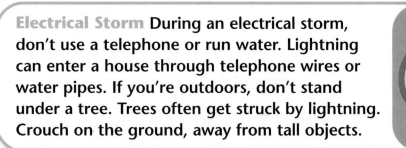

SEQUENCE Tell one thing you can do to keep safe before a hurricane hits.

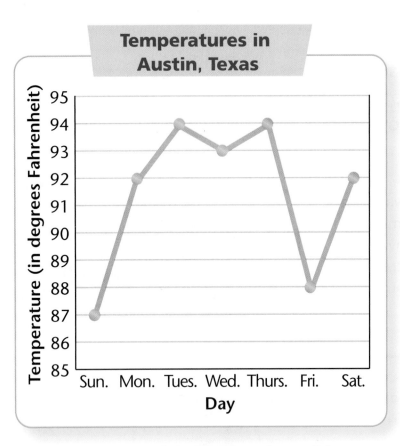

Temperatures in Austin, Texas

Temperature (in degrees Fahrenheit)

Day: Sun. Mon. Tues. Wed. Thurs. Fri. Sat.

▲ Within this week how many times did the temperature rise? drop?

Weather

Knowing what the weather is will help you be prepared. If you want to go on a picnic, it's a good idea to check a weather report. Listening to the weather on TV or radio can also help you decide how to dress. On some cold days you might need to wear a sweater. However, on warm days it might be best to wear short sleeves.

DRAW CONCLUSIONS Suppose you were in Austin, Texas, during the week shown on the graph. How would you dress?

Lesson 3 Summary and Review

❶ **Summarize with Vocabulary**
Use vocabulary and other terms from this lesson to complete the statements.

A _____ is an event that causes widespread damage and may affect many people. Listening to warnings about weather disasters can help keep you _____. Violent acts that some people do to get what they want are called

_____.

❷ **Critical Thinking** You are talking on the phone to a friend. You see lightning. What should you do?

❸ How does putting boards over windows help prevent injury during a hurricane?

❹ (Focus Skill) **SEQUENCE** Draw and complete this graphic organizer to show the steps in being safe during an earthquake.

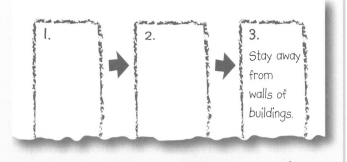

1.

2.

3. Stay away from walls of buildings.

❺ **Write to Inform—Description**
Write a paragraph or two that describes each type of weather disaster you may have experienced.

ACTIVITIES

Science

How Far Away Is Lightning?

Use a watch with a second hand to count the seconds between the time you see a flash of lightning and the time you hear thunder. To find how many miles you are from the lightning, divide the number of seconds by five.

Literature

Write a Story
Read a story about a person who is in a disaster. Write a story about how you would feel if you were in a disaster. Suggest some ways you could handle your feelings.

Technology Project

As you learn the main ideas in this chapter, make a list of at least six rules for keeping you and your family safe. Use a camera to take pictures that show each rule. Paste the pictures on poster board. Label each picture.

GO ONLINE For more activities, visit The Learning Site.
www.harcourtschool.com/health

Home & Community

Home Safety Search
Research home safety hazards. Make a chart of the information you find. Talk about the hazards with your family. Help an adult in your family correct the fire hazards that you find in your home.

Career Link

Meteorologist A meteorologist is someone who studies weather and makes weather predictions. Suppose you are a meteorologist. What information would you give in your weather report? Write what you would say in a weather report. Then find the information about today's weather. Read your weather report to the class.

Chapter Review and Test Preparation

Reading Skill

SEQUENCE

Draw and then use this graphic organizer to answer questions 1–3.

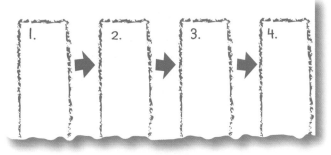

1 What is the first thing you would do in escaping from a fire in your home?

2 What two things would you do next?

3 What is the last thing you would do?

Use Vocabulary

If the sentence is true, write *true*. If the sentence is false, replace the underlined part with a word or words that will make the sentence true.

4 You need to be prepared for an <u>emergency</u> so you can get help quickly.

5 If your clothing catches on fire, you should <u>run and jump</u>.

6 Home products can become <u>useful</u> if they are used in the wrong way.

7 <u>Electricity</u> is a form of energy that can produce light, heat, and motion.

8 A <u>disaster</u> is an event that causes widespread damage.

Check Understanding

Choose the letter of the correct answer.

9 If you and your family practice fire _____, you will know what to do during a fire. (p. 126)
  A routes   **C** drills
  B skills   **D** alarms

10 _____ carry electricity throughout your home. (p. 130)
  F Microwaves
  G Electrical cords
  H Poisons
  J Electrical plugs

11 What should you do if you see a poison within the reach of a younger child? (p. 128)
  A Move the poison.
  B Call 911.
  C Chase the child away.
  D Tell a parent or a trusted adult.

12 Which of these signs means that the person is choking? (p. 133)

F    **H**

G    **J**

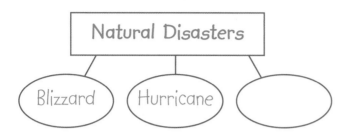

Natural Disasters
- Blizzard
- Hurricane
- ( )

13 Which word would **NOT** belong in this graphic organizer? (pp. 136–137)
A Tornado
C Earthquake
B Car crash
D Electrical storm

14 Which of these activities is a safe way to use electricity? (p. 130)
F Plug only one thing into an outlet.
G Use the telephone during a thunderstorm.
H Turn on a radio with wet hands.
J Run cords under a carpet.

15 What should this girl do? (p. 131)
A Ask an adult to help clean up the broken glass.
B Leave the glass on the floor.
C Clean up the glass.
D Ask her little sister to clean up the glass.

Think Critically

16 Suppose that you didn't go to the meeting place after you escaped from your burning house. What might happen to someone else because of this?

17 You hear on the radio that a tornado is heading toward where you live. You know that a deaf neighbor is home alone. What should you do?

Apply Skills

18 **BUILDING GOOD CHARACTER**
Citizenship You get on the school bus one morning. A group of your friends are standing up in the back of the bus making a lot of noise. They wave for you to join them. Use what you know about obeying rules and laws for safety to help you write about how to be a good citizen in this situation.

19 **LIFE SKILLS**
Communicate An adult falls in the house. She can't get up and is in pain. Use what you know about communicating in emergencies to write about getting help for this person.

Write About Health

20 Write to Inform—Explanation
Describe an emergency. Tell what a person should do in the emergency.

Preventing Disease

Reading Skill

Focus Skill

SEQUENCE To sequence is to list events in the order in which they take place. Use the Reading in Health Handbook on pages 290–291 and this graphic organizer to help you read the health facts in this chapter.

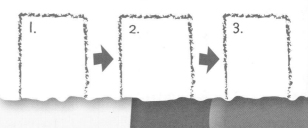

Sequence

1. → 2. → 3.

Health Graph

INTERPRET DATA Water is important to your health. An average apple has about half a cup of water. Which has more water—a banana or an apple?

Water in Fruits

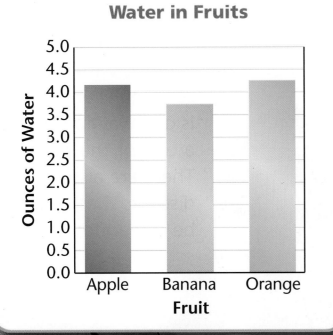

Daily Physical Activity

Being physically active can help prevent some diseases.

Be Active!
Use the selection **Track 7, Movin' and Groovin'**, to beef up your body's protection.

145

Learning About Disease

Disease

Jamal isn't feeling well. His head aches. His throat hurts. Jamal's father takes his temperature. It is higher than it should be. A temperature higher than normal is a *fever*. Jamal's dad says, "You have symptoms of the flu."

A **symptom** (SIMP•tuhm) is a sign that something is wrong in the body. A fever, a headache, and a sore throat can be symptoms of the flu. An illness such as the flu is a disease. A **disease** (dih•ZEEZ) is something that causes the body not to work normally.

Some diseases are spread from person to person. Coughing without covering your mouth is one way to spread a cold or the flu. There are also diseases that cannot be spread to others.

Health & Technology

Modern fever thermometers like the one Jamal's dad is using have replaced thermometers made of glass and mercury. Most have plastic covers, which make them safer. They measure temperatures quickly.

Stacy has an illness that can't be spread to others. It has caused her to have a disability. It keeps her from walking. She uses a wheelchair to get around. A *disability* is a condition that keeps someone from doing some things that a person without that disability might be able to do.

A disability cannot be spread to another person. You should treat friends with diseases and disabilities the same way you treat any of your friends.

SEQUENCE List two things Jamal's dad might do after he takes Jamal's temperature.

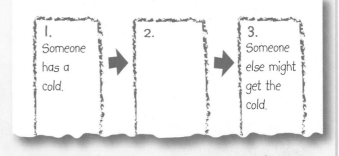

▼ Disabilities cannot be spread to others. Even though Stacy cannot walk, there are many things she can do.

Lesson 1 Summary and Review

❶ Summarize with Vocabulary
Use vocabulary and other terms from this lesson to complete the statements.

A _____ is something that causes the body not to work normally. Signs of a disease are called _____. A body temperature that is higher than normal is a _____.

❷ List two activities you could enjoy with someone who is unable to participate in physical activities.

❸ Critical Thinking Think of a disease that you or someone else has had. What were the symptoms?

❹ SEQUENCE Draw and complete this graphic organizer.

1. Someone has a cold.	→	2.	→	3. Someone else might get the cold.

❺ Write to Inform—Narration
Write a personal story of a time when you had an illness that lasted a few days. Include information on your symptoms.

LESSON 2

Diseases You Can Catch

Lesson Focus

Bacteria and viruses are two kinds of pathogens that cause disease.

Why Learn This?

You can use what you learn to keep from getting a disease.

Vocabulary

communicable disease
pathogens
bacteria
virus

Types of Pathogens

You might know someone who has had a cold this year. A cold is a communicable disease. A **communicable disease** (kuh•MYOO•nih•kuh•buhl) is a disease that can spread from one person to another. Communicable diseases are caused by germs called **pathogens** (PATH•uh•juhnz). A sneeze or cough can spread pathogens to others.

Two kinds of pathogens cause most communicable diseases. One kind is bacteria. **Bacteria** (bak·TIR·ee·uh) are very simple living things. Each is just one cell. You can see bacteria only with a microscope.

Bacteria live in soil, on plants, and in water. They are on the surfaces of most things we touch. Some bacteria can cause disease. When they get into your body, they can make more bacteria. They cause you to become ill.

Another type of pathogen is viruses. A **virus** (VY·ruhs) is one of the tiniest pathogens. Viruses are much smaller than bacteria. They grow in your body's cells. They also cause disease by destroying the cells they use.

SEQUENCE What happens after a virus gets into a cell?

Did You Know?
Viruses cannot be seen with an ordinary microscope. They are so small that you need an electron microscope to see them.

AH CHOO!

Quick Activity

Locate Pathogens Look at the pictures on these two pages. List some ways that pathogens might be spread and how they can be avoided.

Communicable Diseases

Lilly has a communicable disease caused by a type of bacteria. She has a fever and a sore throat. Her doctor says she has strep throat.

When you have a cold, you have a communicable disease caused by a virus. You may have a stuffy nose, a scratchy throat, and a cough. You may even have a fever. Colds usually last about a week.

The flu is also caused by a virus. When you have the flu, you may have many of the same symptoms as when you have a cold. You may also have chills, fever, and body aches. The flu can make you feel very tired. It usually lasts about a week.

COMPARE AND CONTRAST
How are a strep throat and the flu alike? How are they different?

◄Resting is one way to help your body get better.

Other Health Problems That Can Spread

Another common health problem that can spread is head lice. Head lice are very small insects that crawl on the skin and hair. The head becomes very itchy, and tiny red bumps appear near the root of the hair on the head.

If head lice make their home in someone's hair, the person must use a special shampoo that kills the insects. A fine-toothed comb can help remove most of the eggs.

SUMMARIZE List two symptoms that might happen if someone gets head lice.

▼ Don't share hats, combs, or brushes.

Lesson 2 Summary and Review

❶ Summarize with Vocabulary
Use vocabulary from this lesson to complete the statements.

A disease caught from someone else is a _____. These diseases are caused by _____. A cold is caused by a _____. Strep throat is caused by _____.

❷ Critical Thinking Why is it important to learn about communicable diseases?

❸ Name three communicable diseases and some of their symptoms.

❹ (Focus Skill) SEQUENCE Draw and complete this graphic organizer to show what happens after a virus gets inside your body.

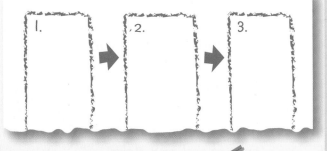

❺ Write to Inform—How-To
Write two steps to take if head lice get into a person's hair.

Fighting Disease

Lesson Focus

Many diseases can be prevented or treated.

Why Learn This?

You can use what you learn to help keep yourself and others healthy.

Vocabulary

immunity
vaccine
medicine

Ways to Prevent Disease

Your body has ways to fight disease. All the parts of your body work hard to fight pathogens that get into your body. Your skin helps keep pathogens from getting into your blood. Sometimes a pathogen gets past the skin's protection.

Staying away from people who have a communicable disease is one way to stay healthy. Another very important way to stay well is by washing your hands often with soap and water.

Preventing Disease

- Wash your hands often.
- Stay away from people who have a communicable disease.
- Cover your mouth or nose when you cough or sneeze.
- Don't share anything that you have put in your mouth or near your nose.
- Don't rub your eyes or nose with dirty hands.
- Get regular physical activity.
- Get plenty of rest and sleep.
- Wash common objects, such as doorknobs, to remove pathogens.

▼ Wash your hands often to help prevent getting a communicable disease.

▼ Marissa and her mom see that it's time for Marissa's annual checkup at the doctor's office.

▲ Marissa cooperates while she gets a vaccine.

Your body has another way to fight disease. Certain substances in the body give you immunity to some diseases. **Immunity** (ih•MYOON•uh•tee) is the body's ability to fight off certain pathogens. You can get immunity by having a disease. This way you will not get that disease again.

Another way to get immunity is through a vaccine. A **vaccine** (vak•SEEN) is a substance given to keep you from getting a certain kind of disease. Most vaccines are given by shots.

DRAW CONCLUSIONS Why is it important to plan for and go to annual checkups?

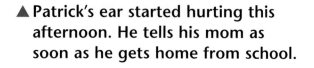

▲ Patrick's ear started hurting this afternoon. He tells his mom as soon as he gets home from school.

▲ Patrick's mom gives him some medicine for his earache and tells him to rest.

Treating Diseases

Before a disease can be identified and treated, health-care workers must know what the symptoms are. Always tell a parent, teacher, or caregiver when you feel ill. Then you will get the care you need.

Diseases are treated in different ways. Many diseases, such as colds and flu, are treated by resting in bed and drinking liquids. Sometimes diseases are treated with medicines. A **medicine** is a substance used to treat an illness. Medicines may be liquids, powders, creams, sprays, or pills.

Fever is a symptom of many communicable diseases. To bring your temperature back to normal, an adult may give you a fever medicine. Some fever medicines are safe for children to take. However, one kind—aspirin—is not safe for children. It can cause a serious illness in children. Remember to take medicine only when a parent or other trusted adult gives it to you. The adult should read the labels or talk with a doctor to decide which medicine to use, how much to give you, and how often you need it.

▲ After taking the medicine and resting, Patrick feels much better.

MAIN IDEA AND DETAILS Diseases are treated in different ways. List two ways diseases can be treated.

Lesson 3 Summary and Review

1 **Summarize with Vocabulary**

Use vocabulary from this lesson to complete the statements.

Your body's ability to fight disease is _____. One way you can keep from getting a certain kind of disease is by receiving a _____ for that disease. When you get ill, you may be given a _____ to treat your illness.

2 **Critical Thinking** Why are symptoms important?

3 List two ways to keep from spreading a communicable disease.

4 **(Focus Skill)** **SEQUENCE** Draw and complete the graphic organizer to show what you should do if you have symptoms of a disease, such as earache, chills, and a sore throat.

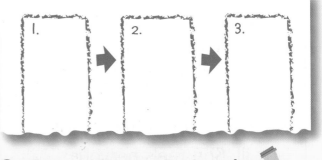

5 **Write to Inform—Explanation**

Write an ad informing others how to avoid getting a communicable disease.

Manage Stress
To Control Disease

We all feel stress sometimes. Something that we must deal with may make us feel worried, nervous, or tense. Stress can affect how well our bodies fight disease. Learning the steps to **Manage Stress** can help keep you healthy.

These four steps can help you manage the stress you might feel in many situations.

1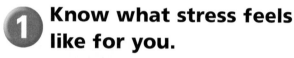
Know what stress feels like for you.

2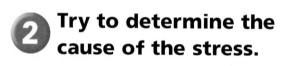
Try to determine the cause of the stress.

Bailey's stomach hurts, but she isn't ill. She feels nervous.

Bailey realizes that she keeps thinking about an oral report that she must give to her class.

3 Talk with someone you trust about the way you are feeling.

Bailey decides to take a walk with her mom and her dog. She talks with her mom about her feelings.

4 Visualize yourself doing well in a stressful situation.

Bailey is prepared, and she knows she will do a great job.

Problem Solving

Roy has a big math test in three days. He is nervous and afraid he won't do well. Use the steps to **Manage Stress** and what you know about caring for your health to help Roy make a study schedule.

How does making a schedule show that Roy is being responsible?

Diseases You Can't Catch

Lesson Focus
Some diseases are not spread by pathogens.

Why Learn This?
You can understand more about diseases that cannot be spread.

Vocabulary
noncommunicable
 disease
allergy
asthma
diabetes
cancer

Noncommunicable Diseases

Communicable diseases are caused by pathogens and spread from one person to another. Diseases that are not caused by pathogens are noncommunicable. A **noncommunicable disease** (nahn•kuh•MYOO•nih•kuh•buhl) is a disease that cannot be spread from one person to another. You may know someone with a noncommunicable disease. Some examples of noncommunicable diseases are allergies, asthma, diabetes, and cancer.

COMPARE AND CONTRAST How are communicable and noncommunicable diseases alike? How are they different?

Quick Activity

Identify Causes of Allergies Look at the drawing on these two pages. Name the common things in the picture that may cause an allergy.

Allergies

One common noncommunicable disease is an allergy. An **allergy** (AL•er•jee) is the body's reaction to a certain thing that is harmless to many other people. Allergies may have mild symptoms such as sneezing, watery eyes, or an itchy rash. However, if the symptoms are very bad, a doctor must treat the person's allergies.

Some people are allergic to nothing or to just one thing. Others are allergic to many things. People may also be allergic to certain foods.

If you have an allergy to something, your doctor may tell you to stay away from it or may give you a medicine to help the symptoms go away. Sometimes people get allergy shots to reduce their symptoms.

MAIN IDEA AND DETAILS List three ways people cope with allergies.

159

Asthma

Asthma (AZ•muh) is a disease that causes people to have difficulty breathing. Asthma episodes, or *attacks*, are usually caused by allergies, some kinds of exercise, or an illness. Symptoms include coughing and difficulty breathing. Sometimes when a person with asthma breathes during an episode, you can hear a squeaky sound called wheezing.

A person with asthma should always follow his or her doctor's advice. The doctor can give the patient an inhaler to help him or her breathe. *You should never share an inhaler or other medicines with other people—even if they have the same symptoms!*

DRAW CONCLUSIONS **Why is it important never to share medicines, even if the other person has the same symptoms?**

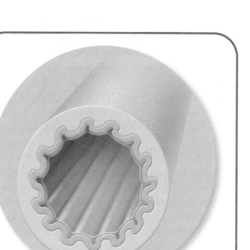

The healthy airway at the top allows enough air to get in and out of the lungs. During an asthma episode, lung airways become very narrow, making breathing difficult.

Diabetes

Diabetes (dy•uh•BEET•eez) is a noncommunicable disease that prevents the body from using sugar properly. The sugar in foods you eat is needed by your body's cells for energy. Sometimes the sugar isn't used by the cells and stays in the person's blood. The cells do not get the energy they need.

A person who has diabetes usually must eat a special diet. The person also might take medicine to help his or her body use the sugar for energy.

COMPARE AND CONTRAST How are diabetes and asthma the same and different?

Consumer Activity

Access Valid Health Information Choose a disease you would like to learn more about. Find out the symptoms of the disease and what treatments might be available.

▼ Rosa is on the swim team. She has asthma. Rosa follows her doctor's advice about caring for her health. Rosa's illness doesn't stop her swimming success!

▼ Rick has cancer. His friend Dave knows that he cannot get cancer from Rick. They still enjoy many of the activities they have always enjoyed together.

Cancer

Another noncommunicable disease is cancer. **Cancer** is a disease in which the body makes cells that are not normal. The cancer cells multiply very quickly. They take over the normal body cells. Many kinds of cancer can be treated when the cancer is found early. If you ever have unusual symptoms or marks on your body, tell a parent or another trusted adult right away.

SUMMARIZE Explain why it is important to tell a family member or another trusted adult if you are having any unusual symptoms.

Lesson 4 Summary and Review

❶ Summarize with Vocabulary

Use vocabulary from this lesson to complete the statements.

A disease that cannot be spread from one person to another is a _____ disease. An _____ is a reaction to a substance by sneezing, itchy eyes, or a rash. If a person has difficulty breathing and coughs and wheezes, he or she may have _____. A disease in which the body can't use sugar correctly is _____. _____ is the fast growth of unusual cells.

❷ Critical Thinking Why would someone with diabetes feel tired?

❸ Name four noncommunicable diseases.

❹ (Focus Skill) SEQUENCE Draw and complete the graphic organizer to show what happens when someone gets an asthma attack.

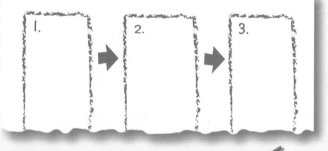

❺ Write to Inform—Explanation
Write a paragraph explaining why people should not use medicines that aren't prescribed for them.

Caring

Showing Concern for Others

When you don't feel well or have been hurt, how do you like others around you to act? How about if you're trying to deal with a difficult situation? Most of us would be sad, or our feelings would be hurt, if others acted as if they didn't care how we felt.

People show concern in many ways. Some might say, "How's it going?" Others might organize a collection of food and clothing for people in need. Your best guide in how to treat others is to treat them as you'd like to be treated in a similar situation.

What could you do for someone who has been hurt? Here are a few suggestions.

- **Bring flowers.**
- **Make a get-well card or send a cheerful e-mail message.**
- **Carry a lunch tray.**
- **Hold a door open.**
- **Play a board game with someone who is unable to play physical games.**

Activity

This week, try to notice how other people are feeling. If someone seems a little down, try to cheer up the person or do a favor for him or her. Make a note in a journal on how it feels to help others.

163

LESSON 5

Staying Healthy

Lesson Focus

Having a healthful lifestyle can help you fight disease.

Why Learn This?

You can use what you learn to keep your body well.

Vocabulary

abstinence

Eat a Healthful Diet

The foods you choose to eat are important to a healthful lifestyle. Healthful food gives your body energy. It also gives your body the things it needs to grow and to fight disease.

If you choose foods that are not healthful, you may have less energy, gain extra weight, and catch communicable diseases more easily. If you eat a lot of foods low in fiber and high in fats, sugar, and salt, you may increase your risk of developing some noncommunicable diseases, too.

CAUSE AND EFFECT What is an effect of eating a healthful diet?

Quick Activity

Identify Healthful Foods Which of these foods would be good choices for a healthful breakfast? List some other healthful breakfast choices.

164

▼ Exercise can be activities with friends and family.

▲ Exercise can be playing with your dog.

▲ Exercise can be done at school.

Exercise Often

Exercise can help you in many ways. It makes your muscles, heart, and lungs stronger. It helps your body use food. It helps your body fight disease.

When you are stressed, you may have a headache, stomachache, or trouble sleeping. Exercise can help make the symptoms of stress go away. It can help you feel calmer. If you exercise regularly, your body will handle stress better.

DRAW CONCLUSIONS How can exercise strengthen your heart and lungs?

Personal Health Plan

Real-Life Situation
Suppose you are worried about a test in school.
Real-Life Plan
List three exercises you could do to handle the stress.

Life Skills

Refuse Deborah's mom has asthma. A neighbor who is visiting asks Deborah's mom if she may smoke in the house. Write a refusal for Deborah's mom to use.

Avoid Tobacco

Using tobacco is not healthful. People who smoke are more likely to catch diseases, such as colds and flu, than those who don't smoke. People who use tobacco often have problems with their teeth and gums. Tobacco use can cause lung cancer, other lung diseases, and heart disease.

To be healthy, you must practice abstinence from tobacco. **Abstinence** (AB•stuh•nuhns) means not doing a certain thing. Choosing not to use tobacco is one of the best things you can do for your health.

MAIN IDEA AND DETAILS **List three health problems caused by tobacco use.**

Lesson 5 Summary and Review

❶ Summarize with Vocabulary

Use vocabulary and other terms from this lesson to complete the statements.

If you have a diet that is not healthful, you may catch _____ diseases easily. If you _____ regularly, your body will handle stress better. To be healthy, you must practice _____ from tobacco.

❷ Critical Thinking Why is it important to manage stress in order to fight disease?

❸ What would you tell someone who thinks smoking is cool?

❹ SEQUENCE Draw and complete this graphic organizer to show what happens when someone feeling stress does a form of exercise he or she enjoys.

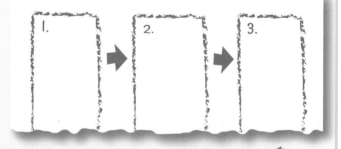

❺ Write to Inform—Description
Write a paragraph to describe how a healthful lifestyle helps a person fight disease.

ACTIVITIES

Language Arts

Poster With a partner, make a poster showing a rhyme that discourages others from smoking.

Physical Education

Exercise Journal Keep track of the exercise you do this week. Make a table with two columns. In the left-hand column, write activities you do each day. In the right-hand column, write how much time you spend doing each activity.

Activities	Time
• walk dog	– 20 min.
• ride bike to school	– 10 min. each way

Technology Project

As you learn the main ideas in this chapter, make a list of some diseases and their causes. Use a computer to make a slide presentation. If a computer is not available, make colorful posters to present the information.

GO ONLINE For more activities, visit The Learning Site.
www.harcourtschool.com/health

Home & Community

Vaccine Ad Make an advertisement that describes the importance of getting vaccines. Display the ad in your classroom.

Career Link

Lab Technician Suppose that you are a lab technician. You receive a cotton swab from a doctor's office. After doing some tests, you discover that there are bacteria on the swab. The bacteria are the kind that can cause strep throat. Write a report explaining whether the disease is communicable or noncommunicable and how you know.

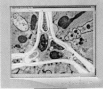

Focus Skill Reading Skill

SEQUENCE

Draw this graphic organizer, and use it to answer questions 1 and 2.

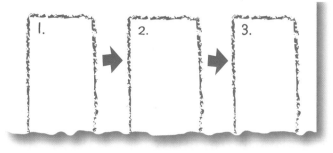

1. In the first box write *Frequent exercise.* Complete the next two boxes.
2. In the first box write *Smoking.* Complete the next two boxes.

Use Vocabulary

Match each term in Column B with its meaning in Column A.

Column A	Column B
3 Ability to fight a disease	A vaccine
	B abstinence
4 Substance given to keep you from getting a certain disease	C immunity
	D medicine
	E symptom
5 A sign that something is wrong in the body	
6 Not doing certain things that will harm your health	
7 Substance used to treat an illness	

Check Understanding

Choose the letter of the correct answer.

8 Communicable diseases are caused by _____. (p. 148)
A medicines
B pathogens
C fever
D exercise

9 Pathogens that cause strep throat are ___. (p. 150)
F viruses
G allergies
H bacteria
J colds

10 Which of the following is a communicable disease? (p. 150)
A cancer   C flu
B asthma   D allergies

11 Coughing, wheezing, and difficulty breathing are symptoms of _____. (p. 160)
F cancer   H head lice
G diabetes   J asthma

12 Which of the following is **NOT** a way to prevent disease? (p. 152)

A    C

B    D

13 What is missing from the graphic organizer below? (pp. 164–166)

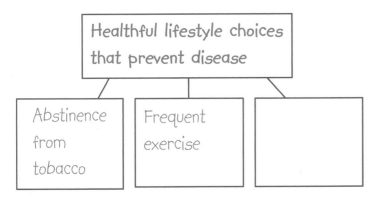

Healthful lifestyle choices that prevent disease
- Abstinence from tobacco
- Frequent exercise

F watching television
G going to school with flu
H healthful food choices
J not washing hands often

14 An allergy is an example of a _____ . (p. 158)
A noncommunicable disease
B vaccine
C medicine
D communicable disease

15 _____ is a way to prevent disease and is usually given as a shot. (p. 153)
F viruses
G vaccine
H strep throat
J medicine

Think Critically

16 Jada has chicken pox. A virus causes chicken pox. Could Jada spread chicken pox to others? Explain.

17 Trey eats many high-fat foods and rarely exercises. Explain how and why he should change his lifestyle.

Apply Skills

18 **BUILDING GOOD CHARACTER**
Caring Your classmate has a broken leg. What can you do to help him at school and show your concern for him?

19 **LIFE SKILLS**
Managing Stress Suppose you are to act in a school play next month. You want to be in the play but are nervous about being on stage. How can you manage your stress to help you feel comfortable about being on stage?

Write About Health

20 **Write to Inform—Explanation**
Explain how eating healthful foods can help you fight disease.

8 Medicines and Other Drugs

Reading Skill

DRAW CONCLUSIONS Sometimes you have to use information from the passage plus what you already know to draw a conclusion. Use the Reading in Health Handbook on pages 284–285 and this graphic organizer to help you read the health facts in this chapter.

Draw Conclusions

What I Read	+	What I Know	=	Conclusion:

Health Graph

INTERPRET DATA Caffeine is found in many products. About how much more caffeine is found in cola than is found in iced tea?

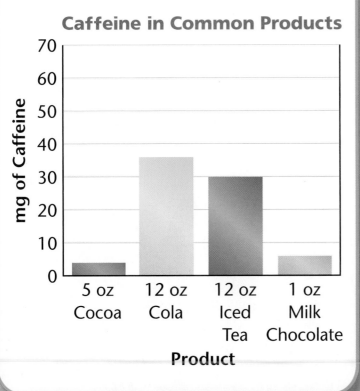

Caffeine in Common Products

Daily Physical Activity

Refusing drugs will help keep you healthy.

 **Be Active!**
Use the selection **Track 8, Jumping and Pumping**, to make your body feel better.

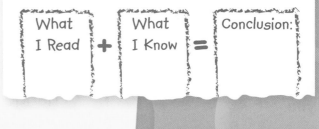

Learning About Drugs

Kinds of Drugs

A **drug** is something other than food that changes the way the body works. Some drugs are **medicines** (MED•uh•suhnz). Medicines can help keep you from getting ill. Some can cure you when you are ill. Medicines can also help you feel better.

Medicines are helpful, but other kinds of drugs can harm you. Some foods and drinks, such as chocolate, coffee, and many soft drinks, have a drug in them called **caffeine** (kaf•EEN). Caffeine can make people feel more awake. Too much caffeine can be harmful.

Did You Know?

Long ago, Native Americans found that drinking tea made from the bark of a willow tree took away pain. The bark contains the same chemical found in aspirin.

▼ Medicines can help you when you are ill or in pain.

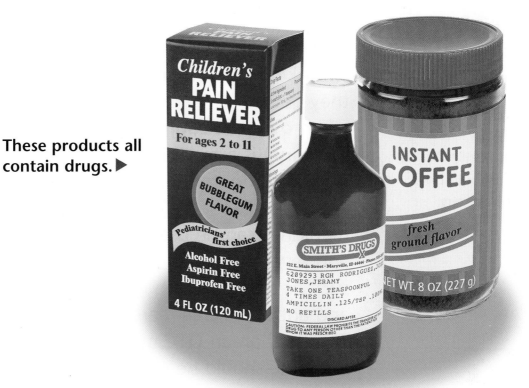

These products all contain drugs. ▶

Drugs change the ways people think, feel, and act. They can make people very sick. Because they can be harmful, many drugs are illegal. It is against the law to buy, sell, have, or use them.

Many products used in homes give off dangerous fumes. Some people breathe the fumes on purpose. The fumes are poisons that can cause illness, brain damage, or even death.

DRAW CONCLUSIONS Why is it important not to use cleaning products without the permission or help of an adult?

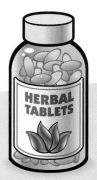

Myth and Fact

Myth: Herbal medicines are safer than medicines from a pharmacy.

Fact: Though herbal medicines are "natural," many of them contain very strong drugs. In fact, some of the strongest drugs come from nature. Any medicine can be harmful if it is used incorrectly.

Personal Health Plan ▶

Real-Life Situation
Suppose you wake up in the morning and you feel sick.

Real-Life Plan
Make a list of the things you should do when this happens.

Over-the-Counter Medicines

When you are sick, how do adults know what kind of medicine you need? Where do they get it?

An **over-the-counter medicine** (OTC medicine) is a medicine that an adult can buy without a doctor's order. Drugstores and grocery stores sell OTC medicines. OTC medicines can be used to treat minor pains and fever. Some can be used to treat an illness such as a cold. Cough medicine, allergy pills, and antibiotic cream are some OTC medicines. The label on an OTC medicine tells what the medicine should be used for. It gives directions for using the medicine safely.

 DRAW CONCLUSIONS **Why must a trusted adult read and follow a label's directions before giving you medicine?**

▼ OTC medicines can treat minor problems, like this girl's cough.

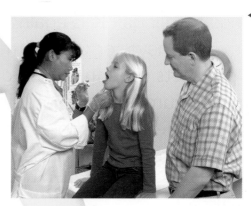

◀ If an OTC medicine does not work, a trip to a doctor may be needed.

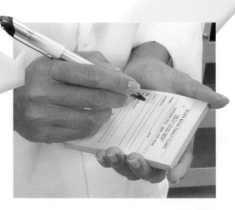

The doctor may write an order for a prescription medicine. ▶

Prescription Medicines

A **prescription medicine** (prih•SKRIP•shuhn) is a drug that must be ordered by a doctor. A doctor writes the order, called a *prescription*. Then a pharmacist (FAHR•muh•sist) fills the order. The doctor or pharmacist explains exactly how to use the medicine.

Prescription medicines are strong. Like all medicines, they must be used correctly. They may have more side effects than OTC medicines. A **side effect** is an unwanted change in the body caused by a medicine. Becoming dizzy, sleepy, or sick to your stomach are examples of side effects.

COMPARE AND CONTRAST How are over-the-counter medicines and prescription medicines alike? How are they different?

Information Alert!

From Prescription to OTC Over time, many prescription drugs are found to be safe enough to be sold over the counter.

GO ONLINE **For the most up-to-date information, visit The Learning Site. www.harcourtschool.com/health**

▲ A doctor's prescription must be taken to a pharmacy.

▼ The pharmacist fills the doctor's written prescription.

Consumer Activity

Access Valid Health Information Use the Internet or other sources to find out how much caffeine is in soft drinks. Make a list of at least five soft drinks. Next to each one, write how many milligrams of caffeine the soft drink has.

Caffeine

Do you enjoy iced tea, chocolate, and cola drinks? Many people do. But watch out! Many of these items contain caffeine. Some OTC medicines have caffeine, too. Caffeine speeds up the heart.

It is not harmful to take in a small amount of caffeine. Many adults drink coffee in the morning to help them feel more alert. But large amounts of caffeine can make an adult feel jittery. Children are affected by smaller amounts. Too much caffeine can strain the heart and upset the stomach.

It is hard for people who use a lot of caffeine to stop. When they don't have caffeine, they feel tired and get upset easily. They might also get headaches.

Many people drink a lot of soft drinks with caffeine or eat a lot of chocolate. They may not know that they are taking caffeine into their bodies. If you know which foods have it, you can avoid caffeine.

If you often eat or drink foods with caffeine, try to eat or drink foods that do not have caffeine. You might drink milk or water instead of soda. You might eat an apple instead of chocolate cake.

SUMMARIZE What are the effects of caffeine on the body?

Myth and Fact

Myth: The only soft drinks that contain caffeine are colas.
Fact: Though caffeine occurs naturally in colas, it is added to many soft drinks, including some brands of orange soda, root beer, and lemon-lime soda.

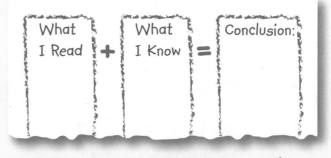

Lesson 1 Summary and Review

❶ Summarize with Vocabulary
Use vocabulary from this lesson to complete the statements.

Medicines and other _____ change the way the body works. _____ is a drug found in chocolate and in cola drinks. Drugs that a doctor does not need to order are called _____ medicines. A doctor must order other drugs, called _____ medicines.

❷ Critical Thinking Can a medicine help you even if it does not cure you? Give an example.

❸ List four foods or drinks that contain caffeine.

❹ (Focus Skill) **DRAW CONCLUSIONS** Draw and complete this graphic organizer to show why it is important to read and follow labels on medicines.

What I Read	+	What I Know	=	Conclusion:

❺ Write to Inform—Explanation
Often a prescribed medicine is more helpful than an OTC medicine. Explain why a doctor might decide to write an order for a drug.

Using Medicines Safely

Lesson Focus

Medicine that is used in the wrong way can harm the body.

Why Learn This?

For medicines to be helpful, you must learn to use them correctly.

▼ Medicines can help you get well or relieve symptoms when you are sick.

How Medicines Help

Some medicines can cure an illness. Others can help you feel better while you are ill. A doctor might give you a medicine called an antibiotic. Antibiotics kill the bacteria that might cause an earache or a sore throat.

Some medicines don't cure illnesses like a cold or the flu. But they can take away symptoms. Some medicines can lower a fever caused by the flu. One medicine someone your age should **NOT** take is aspirin. Aspirin is safe only for adults. It can cause an illness in children that can lead to death.

⭐ Focus Skill **DRAW CONCLUSIONS Why should people take medicines that will not cure an illness?**

Safety Rules for Medicine Use

Medicines can be harmful if they are used in the wrong way. Always remember to follow these rules when using a medicine.

- Never take a medicine on your own. Only a parent or another trusted adult should give you medicine.

- An adult should read and follow exactly the directions on the label. Leave the labels on all medicines.

- Tell an adult if you feel side effects after taking a medicine. A side effect might be dizziness, an upset stomach, or a headache.

- Never take someone else's medicine or share your medicine.

- Don't use old medicines. Check the date on the label.

- Keep medicines on high shelves in locked cabinets.

- Keep medicines away from small children.

Quick Activity

Interpret Rules Read the Safety Rules for Medicine Use. Then look at the picture on page 178. Describe how the people here are following the safety rules.

DRAW CONCLUSIONS Why should a trusted adult make decisions about medicines for you?

Medicine

ALLERGY Medicine

20 Tablets

Drug Facts

Active ingredient (in each tablet)
Loratadine 10 mg................................. Purpose
Antihistamine

Uses temporarily relieves these symptoms due to hay fever or other upper respiratory allergies:
- runny nose
- itchy, watery eyes
- sneezing
- itching of the nose or throat

Warnings
Do not use if you have ever had an allergic reaction to this product or any of its ingredients.

Ask a doctor before use if you have liver or kidney disease. Your doctor should determine if you need a different dose.

When using this product do not take more than directed. Taking more than directed may cause drowsiness.

Stop use and ask a doctor if an allergic reaction to this product occurs. Seek medical help right away.

Drug Facts (continued)

Keep out of reach of children. In case of overdose, get medical help or contact a Poison Control Center right away.

Directions

adults and children 6 years and over	1 tablet daily; not more than 1 tablet in 24 hours
children under 6 years of age	ask a doctor
consumers with liver or kidney disease	ask a doctor

Other information
- safety sealed: do not use if the individual blister unit imprinted with is open or torn
- store between 2° and 30° C (36° and 86° F)
- protect from excessive moisture

Inactive ingredients
corn starch, lactose monohydrate, magnesium stearate

Compliance Aids

Compliance means "doing what you are supposed to do." With medicines, this means taking the right medicine, in the right amount, at the right time. There are many "compliance aids" to help people take their medicines properly. For example, people can arrange for a cell phone reminder service to call them when it is time for their medicine.

Different Forms of Medicine

Medicines come in many different forms. There are pills, liquids, sprays, and creams. Some pills should be chewed. Other pills must be swallowed whole. Some liquid medicines, like cough syrups, are meant to be swallowed. Other liquids, creams, and sprays are put on the skin. Still others are injected into the body with a needle.

Medicines can help only if they are used correctly. Always follow the directions of the doctor. Chewable pills should not be swallowed whole. Pills meant to be swallowed should not be chewed. Liquids meant for the skin should not be swallowed. No matter what the form is, an adult should always give you all medicines.

SUMMARIZE What are the different ways of getting medicine into your body?

Lesson 2 Summary and Review

❶ Summarize with Vocabulary

Use terms from this lesson to complete the statements.

A doctor might give you a medicine called an _____ to kill bacteria that make you sick. When taking medicine, you should always report any _____, such as dizziness, to a trusted adult. Children should **NEVER** take _____. It can cause a serious illness in children.

❷ What kinds of information are found on a medicine label?

❸ Critical Thinking Why should medicines be kept away from young children?

❹ (Focus Skill) **DRAW CONCLUSIONS** Draw and complete this graphic organizer to show why you should be careful when taking medicines.

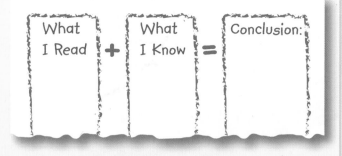

What I Read + What I Know = Conclusion:

❺ Write to Inform—Description
Describe how medicines can be both helpful and harmful.

180

Trustworthiness

Reporting Dangerous Situations

Being trustworthy means that you can be counted on to do the right thing. Follow these rules to show that you are trustworthy.

- **Be honest.**
- **Don't lie, cheat, or steal.**
- **Be reliable—do what you say you will do.**
- **Have the courage to do the right thing.**

Activity

Trustworthiness includes reporting dangerous situations to trusted adults. Practice role-playing with your friends. Suppose you find a package of medicine on the playground at school. What would you do?

Act out these behaviors that show trustworthiness.

- **Do not touch the package.**
- **Tell others around not to touch the package.**
- **Ask a friend to stand guard while you go for help. Your friend can keep others from handling the package.**
- **Tell a trusted adult that you have found something dangerous. Show him or her where it is.**

Harmful and Illegal Drugs

Lesson Focus

There are many harmful drugs. Some are household products that can be misused.

Why Learn This?

Knowing the effects of dangerous drugs and fumes can help you avoid them.

Vocabulary

inhalants
marijuana
cocaine

Inhalants

You have probably heard of some harmful and illegal drugs. Did you know that many products used at home contain harmful drugs?

You walk into the bathroom and know right away that it has just been cleaned. How? You smell the fumes from the cleaning products.

Substances that give off fumes are **inhalants** (in•HAYL•uhnts). Labels on inhalants warn people not to breathe them. The fumes are poisons, and breathing them is dangerous.

ACTIVITY

Life Skills

Communicate

After school, Maya stays at her friend Cicely's house until her mother gets home from work. One day, Cicely's older brother tries to get the girls to breathe in dangerous fumes. Maya does not want to use inhalants, but Cicely is unsure. How can Maya communicate that using inhalants is wrong?

Inhalants have many dangerous side effects.▶

WARNING

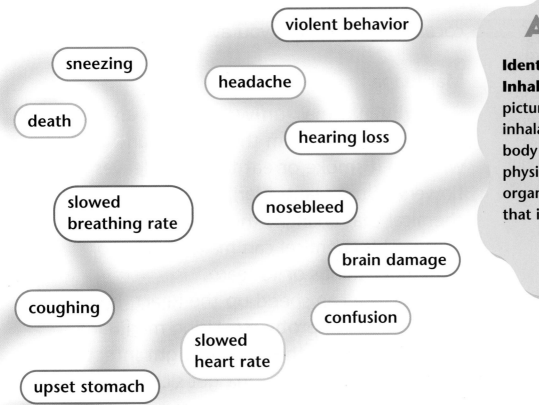

violent behavior

sneezing

headache

death

hearing loss

slowed breathing rate

nosebleed

brain damage

coughing

confusion

slowed heart rate

upset stomach

Quick Activity

Identify Dangers of Inhalants Study the picture showing how inhalants affect the body mentally and physically. List the organs of the body that inhalants affect.

Inhalants change how you see, hear, and feel things. Many people do not think of inhalants as drugs because they are not illegal to have. Household products usually have a caution on the label. These products should be used only for the purpose given. Always use these products in an open, airy place.

Some people breathe in fumes from household products on purpose. This is very dangerous. Many people have died instantly from inhaling dangerous fumes.

 DRAW CONCLUSIONS Some stores will sell products that give off fumes only to adults. Explain why.

Illegal Drugs

Do you know the facts about marijuana and cocaine? Why should you avoid these drugs?

Marijuana

Marijuana (mair•uh•WAH•nuh) is an illegal drug that comes from the hemp plant. People who use it smoke or eat the dried leaves and flowers of the plant. Marijuana contains a chemical that changes the way the brain works. This chemical can make it hard to remember things or to learn.

Marijuana can speed up the heart. It can cause breathing problems. Using marijuana makes it hard for the body to fight infections. People who use marijuana get sick more often than people who do not. When it is smoked, it can cause lung problems such as asthma and cancer, just as smoking tobacco can.

Marijuana comes from the leaves of the hemp plant. It is dangerous and illegal. ▼

▲ This police officer's dog uses its sense of smell to find marijuana and other drugs.

Cocaine

Cocaine (koh•KAYN) is an illegal drug made from the leaves of the coca plant. Most people who use the drug sniff powdered cocaine. Some inject it with a needle. Others smoke a strong form of cocaine called crack.

Cocaine can make the user feel good for a short time. Then the user often feels sad, nervous, confused, angry, or tired. Users need more and more of the drug to get the same feeling back.

Cocaine users may feel dizzy. Cocaine can also cause lung or brain damage. Even one use of cocaine can cause a stroke, heart attack, or death.

CAUSE AND EFFECT What happens to the body of a person who uses marijuana?

Lesson 3 Summary and Review

❶ Summarize with Vocabulary

Use vocabulary and other terms from this lesson to complete the statements.

Substances that give off fumes are _____. A chemical in _____ changes the way the brain works. A strong form of cocaine that is smoked is called _____.

❷ Critical Thinking Why should people turn on a fan when using certain kinds of glue?

❸ What are the harmful effects of cocaine?

❹ DRAW CONCLUSIONS Draw and complete this graphic organizer to show why illegal drugs and inhalants are harmful.

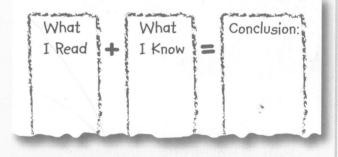

| What I Read | + | What I Know | = | Conclusion: |

❺ Write to Inform—Description

Explain how personal health habits affect both the drug user and others.

REFUSE
Inhalants

Sometimes you have to make decisions about something that can harm your body. Drew sees some cans and bottles on the garage shelf. He is curious and asks his friend Adam to help him explore what is there. "Let's mix these together!" Drew says. How would the steps for **Refusing** keep Adam safe and healthy?

1 **Avoid possible problem situations.**

Adam does not want to touch the cans and bottles on the shelf. The labels show that they have dangerous chemicals inside them.

2 **Say *no* and state your reasons for saying *no*.**

Adam knows that the fumes from the things on the shelf could make the boys sick.

3 Remember a consequence and keep saying *no*.

Adam knows that his family would not want him or his friend touching the cans and bottles.

4 Suggest something else to do.

Adam and Drew decide to play ball instead. By following Adam's family rules, they stay safe.

Problem Solving

Marta is visiting her cousin Joanna. Joanna has found some pills in the bathroom cabinet. She wants Marta to try them with her. Use the steps for **Refusing** to show how Marta should refuse to use the pills. How will her actions show that Marta is responsible?

Reading Skill

DRAW CONCLUSIONS

Draw and then use this graphic organizer to answer questions 1 and 2.

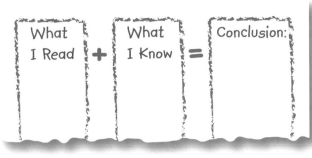

1 Why is reading the labels of OTC medicines important?

2 Why should you avoid the fumes from household products?

Use Vocabulary

Match each term in Column B with its meaning in Column A.

Column A	Column B
3 Medicine that must be ordered by a doctor	**A** caffeine
	B prescription medicine
4 A drug that speeds up the heart	**C** drug
	D refuse
5 Substances that give off fumes	**E** inhalants
6 To say *no*	
7 Something, other than food, that changes the way the body works	

Check Understanding

8 Where should an adult look to find out how much of an OTC medicine to take? (p. 174)

A

C

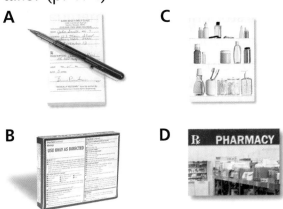

B

D

9 An illegal drug made from the leaves and flowers of the hemp plant is _____. (p. 184)

  F cocaine   **H** an inhalant

  G marijuana   **J** safe at first

10 Rules for medicine safety include _____. (p. 179)

  A not eating before taking it

  B drinking plenty of water with the medicine

  C only taking it from a trusted adult

  D calling your doctor before taking any

11 Marijuana use can cause _____. (p. 184)

  F memory problems   **H** a rash

  G sneezing   **J** a nosebleed

12 Which is **NOT** a way to refuse drugs? (p. 189)

  A ignoring the person

  B saying "Maybe later."

  C suggesting something else to do

  D walking away

13 A person who uses illegal drugs might _____. (p. 188)

  F go to jail   **H** become sick

  G die   **J** all of these

14 A medicine that can be bought without a doctor's order is called _____. (p. 174)

  A an OTC medicine   **C** a pain reliever

  B a prescription   **D** an inhalant

15 What is missing from the graphic organizer? (p. 188)

Cause   Effect

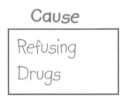 

Refusing Drugs

  F poor grades

  G healthy relationships

  H sickness

  J memory and learning problems

Think Critically

16 Illegal drugs, such as marijuana and cocaine, are harmful. Why do some people use them anyway?

17 Why should you read labels on household products?

Apply Skills

18 **BUILDING GOOD CHARACTER**
Trustworthiness You are home alone after school, and you have a bad headache. Your mother has told you never to take any medicine on your own. But you know that she always gives you two OTC pain reliever tablets when you tell her your head hurts. What behavior would show that you are trustworthy?

19 **LIFE SKILLS**
Refuse You go to a friend's house after school. Your friend's older sister suggests that you inhale the fumes from a can she found in the garage. How do you refuse?

Write About Health

20 **Write to Inform—Explanation**
Explain why staying drug-free now will help you as an adult.

CHAPTER 9

Avoiding Tobacco and Alcohol

Be smoke FREE

NO to alcohol

Focus Skill — Reading Skill

IDENTIFY MAIN IDEA AND DETAILS

The main idea is the most important thought in the passage. Details tell about the main idea. Use the Reading in Health Handbook on pages 288–289 and this graphic organizer to help you read and understand the information in this chapter.

Identify Main Idea and Details

Main Idea:

Detail: | Detail: | Detail:

Health Graph

INTERPRET DATA This graph shows that most adults do not smoke. About 16 percent of adults smoke but want to quit. Suppose that all the adults who wanted to quit smoking did so. What percent of adults would be nonsmokers then?

Who Smokes? Who Does Not?

77% Nonsmoking adults

16% Smoking adults who want to quit

7% Smoking adults who do not want to quit

Daily Physical Activity

Keep healthy by staying fit and avoiding tobacco and alcohol.

Be Active!
Use the selection
Track 9,
Hop to It,
to practice some
healthful activity
choices.

Tobacco and Its Effects

Lesson Focus

Tobacco is a harmful drug.

Why Learn This?

Knowing the dangers of tobacco can help you avoid using it.

Vocabulary

chewing tobacco
smokeless tobacco
nicotine
addiction
tar
cancer
environmental tobacco
 smoke

Learning About Tobacco

You may have seen adults use tobacco products. You may think these products are safe. But did you know that tobacco contains a harmful drug?

Most people who use tobacco smoke it. It can be smoked in a cigarette, a pipe, or a cigar. To make smoking tobacco, the green leaves of the tobacco plant are dried and shredded.

Some people chew small wads of moist tobacco. Moist tobacco for chewing is called **chewing tobacco**. Other people put clumps of powdered or shredded tobacco between the cheek and gum and suck it. These kinds of tobacco are called **smokeless tobacco**.

▼ The tobacco in these products comes from the leaves of the tobacco plant.

Myth and Fact

Myth: **Flavored cigarettes don't have dangerous chemicals the way regular cigarettes do.**

Fact: **Flavored cigarettes are just as dangerous as other cigarettes. Many are even more dangerous.**

PRECAUTIONARY STATEMENTS—HAZARDS
TO HUMANS AND DOMESTIC ANIMALS—
CAUTION

Harmful if swallowed, inhaled, or absorbed
through skin. May cause irritation of eyes, nose,
throat, and skin. Avoid contact with eyes or skin.
Avoid breathing dust. Wash thoroughly with soap
and water after handling. Remove contaminated
clothing and wash before reuse.

STATEMENT OF PRACTICAL TREATMENT

If on Skin: Wash with plenty of soap and water.
If in Eyes: Flush eyes with water for fifteen minutes and get medical attention.
If inhaled: Remove victim to fresh air. Seek medical attention if respiratory irritation occurs or if
breathing becomes difficult.

◀ Farmers and
gardeners use
nicotine to kill
insects and weeds.

All tobacco products have nicotine.
Nicotine is a dangerous drug. People who
use tobacco are putting this drug into their
bodies. Like all drugs, nicotine causes changes
in the body. Some drugs, such as medicines,
cause healthful changes. Nicotine causes
harmful physical and mental changes.

Nicotine is a poison. A few drops of
nicotine can kill an adult. Smaller amounts
harm the body. Many tobacco users mentally
feel the need to keep using tobacco even
when it makes them physically ill. This is
because nicotine can cause addiction.
Addiction is a need to keep using a drug
even when the user wants to stop.

⭐ Focus Skill **MAIN IDEA AND DETAILS** **What are five
kinds of tobacco products?**

Ways Tobacco Affects the Body

Tobacco smoke has more than 4,000 different things in it. Many of these can harm a person's body. You have already learned how harmful nicotine is. Tobacco smoke also has tar in it.

Mouth Smoking causes bad breath. Smokeless tobacco stains teeth. It makes the gums and lips crack and bleed. It can lead to mouth cancer.

Throat Smoking makes a person cough. It can cause throat cancer.

Heart Nicotine makes blood vessels shrink. The heart beats faster and harder. This can lead to heart disease.

Lungs Tar coats a smoker's lungs. Breathing becomes hard. Smokers may die from lung cancer or other lung diseases.

Quick Activity

List Tobacco's Effects List as many harmful effects of tobacco on the body as you can. When you finish with your list, compare it with a classmate's list.

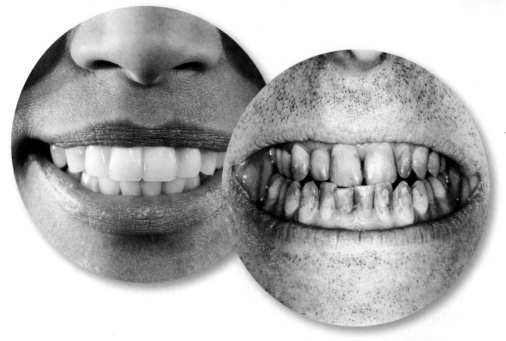

◀ Tobacco can make a mess of your mouth! Tobacco causes yellow teeth, bad breath, cracked lips, and mouth cancer.

Tar is a dark, sticky material. It coats the lungs of people who breathe in tobacco smoke. Tar makes it hard to breathe. Tar in the lungs can lead to lung diseases and cancer. **Cancer** is a disease that makes cells grow wildly, and it can kill a person. Tobacco smoke has more than 50 other things in it that can cause cancer.

SUMMARIZE How can tobacco harm your health?

Did You Know?

Each year, smoking causes about 430,000 deaths. Look at the graph to see how that number compares to deaths by other causes.

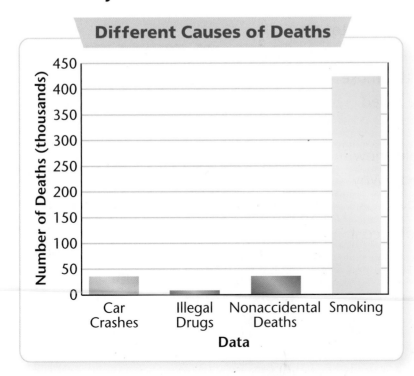

Different Causes of Deaths

Number of Deaths (thousands) / Data

Car Crashes, Illegal Drugs, Nonaccidental Deaths, Smoking

Real-Life Situation
You might go somewhere that does not have no-smoking laws.
Real-Life Plan
Write a plan on how you can avoid ETS.

Ways Tobacco Can Be Harmful to Nonusers

Have you ever been in a room with someone who was smoking? If so, you probably saw smoke in the air. The smoke that fills a room when someone smokes is called **environmental tobacco smoke**, or ETS.

ETS has poisons that can harm people who breathe it—even if they don't smoke at all. People who do not smoke but breathe ETS may get the same diseases as smokers. That is why there are rules against smoking in schools and in other public places.

DRAW CONCLUSIONS **Why should nonsmokers avoid ETS?**

Lesson 1 Summary and Review

1 Summarize with Vocabulary
Use vocabulary from this lesson to complete these statements.

Tobacco contains a harmful drug called _____. A person who is not able to stop using tobacco has an _____. A black, sticky material in cigarette smoke is _____. It can cause a disease called _____.

2 Critical Thinking Most people know that tobacco can harm the body. Why do some people still use tobacco?

3 How can you be harmed by tobacco if you don't smoke?

4 (Focus Skill) **MAIN IDEA AND DETAILS** Draw and complete this graphic organizer to show how tobacco harms the body.

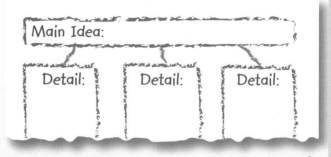

Main Idea:

Detail: Detail: Detail:

5 Write to Express—Business Letter
Write a letter to a business, telling how no-smoking rules can protect people from ETS. The letter should try to get the business not to allow smoking in its building.

Trustworthiness

Do the Right Thing

Trustworthiness means being honest and telling the truth. It means keeping promises. Doing the right thing, even when adults are not around, is part of being trustworthy. Here are some tips for being a trustworthy person:

- **Always follow your parents' rules, even when your parents are not there.**
- **Help your friends follow their parents' rules.**
- **Do not be friends with people who break the law. Remember, it is against the law for people your age to use tobacco and alcohol.**
- **Tell a trusted adult if you see somebody doing something that is against the law or dangerous.**
- **Be honest with your parents.**

Activity

Suppose that your friend Christa is home alone one day. Her parents won't be home for a few hours. Christa calls you on the phone and says she is thinking about smoking a cigarette. Write down any advice you would give Christa about being trustworthy.

Alcohol and Its Effects

Lesson Focus
Alcohol can be a harmful drug.

Why Learn This?
Knowing how dangerous alcohol is can help you refuse to use it.

Vocabulary
alcohol
alcoholism

Learning About Alcohol

You may have seen adults drink alcohol. **Alcohol** is a drug found in beer, liquor, and wine. Like nicotine, alcohol causes changes in the body. An adult who drinks too much alcohol can have health problems. Alcohol is especially harmful to young people because they are still growing.

When a person drinks alcohol, it goes to the stomach and small intestine. Because alcohol does not have to be digested like food, it moves directly into the blood. Once alcohol enters the blood, it travels to all other parts of the body in just a few seconds.

SEQUENCE **Explain the path that alcohol takes in the body.**

ACTIVITY

Life Skills

Communicate
Some people might have problems refusing alcohol. You might be concerned that a family member or close friend is having this problem. If this happens, talk to a trusted adult, such as a school counselor, about your feelings.

▲ Alcohol comes in many different forms.

▲ Every year in the United States, more than 17,000 people die in car crashes due to alcohol.

Ways Alcohol Is Harmful

Even a small amount of alcohol can be harmful. Alcohol keeps the brain and body from growing right. That's why it is illegal for young people to use alcohol.

People who drink alcohol are at risk for injuries. Sometimes they fall down or run into things. Drinking alcohol before driving a car can cause crashes. Drivers who have been drinking can hurt or kill themselves or others. Alcohol also affects the way people act. People who drink alcohol are more likely to feel angry and get into fights.

Drinking alcohol can lead to a disease called **alcoholism** . People who have this disease can't stop using alcohol. They know that alcohol causes problems for them and their family. But they still drink it. They are addicted to alcohol.

Myth and Fact

Myth: Alcoholics always wear dirty clothes and drink in alleys.
Fact: Most alcoholics appear to live normal lives. It is not possible to tell that a person is an alcoholic by the way he or she looks.

CAUSE AND EFFECT **What can be some social effects of drinking alcohol?**

Brain Alcohol affects speech and the way a person moves and sees. It can shut down the brain, causing death.

Heart Alcohol speeds up the heart. It beats faster. Blood pressure goes up. High blood pressure can be dangerous.

Liver The liver tries to break down alcohol. But alcohol stays in the liver and causes damage. This can lead to liver failure and death.

Stomach Alcohol can cause an upset stomach. Heavy drinking can damage the stomach.

Small Intestine Alcohol use can destroy chemicals that digest food.

Alcohol use affects many parts of the body. ▶

Quick
Activity

Label a Diagram
Make an outline of your body on a large piece of paper. Draw lines to the brain, heart, liver, and stomach. Write how alcohol can harm each of these body parts.

Ways Alcohol Affects the Body

Alcohol use affects the body in many ways. It slows the brain and the messages it sends. After drinking alcohol, a person might have trouble walking, speaking, or seeing clearly. Making decisions isn't easy. Paying attention and remembering things become hard, too. Alcohol use can even change your personality. Some people feel sad and others become angry.

People who drink too much often feel sleepy or ill. They get dizzy and have headaches. People who drink too much may feel ill the next day, too.

Some people drink a lot of alcohol for many years. Over time, heavy drinking can harm almost every part of the body. Alcohol can harm the liver, which cleans the blood. Alcohol use can even scar the liver. Then the liver can't clean the blood. A person whose liver stops working may die.

Alcohol can harm the brain, making it hard to think clearly or remember things. A person who doesn't think clearly may make wrong decisions and take risks that a nonuser might not.

DRAW CONCLUSIONS How can alcohol use affect a person mentally?

Lesson 2 Summary and Review

1 Summarize with Vocabulary
Use vocabulary and other terms from this lesson to complete these statements.

Wine and beer contain a drug called _____. The drug goes right into the _____ and spreads quickly to all parts of the body. People who become addicted to alcohol have a disease known as _____.

2 Critical Thinking Why should young people stay alcohol-free?

3 Why might a person who uses alcohol have trouble learning?

4 (Focus Skill) MAIN IDEA AND DETAILS Draw and complete this graphic organizer to show how alcohol harms the body.

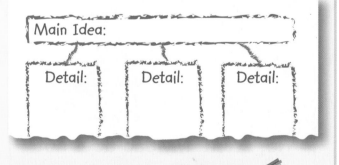

Main Idea:

Detail: Detail: Detail:

5 Write to Inform—Description
Write how alcohol can harm family and social relationships.

Refuse
Alcohol and Tobacco

Beth and Sheila are at the basketball court. Sheila brought her big sister's pack of cigarettes. Sheila thinks smoking looks cool. She wants Beth to try it with her. How can Beth say *no*? Use the steps for **Refusing** to help Beth say *no* to Sheila.

1 Say *no* firmly. State your reasons for saying *no*.

2 Say that you don't want to be sick.

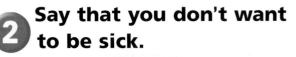

"No, I can't. My dad does not allow me to," Beth says.

"Come on, just try one," Sheila says.
Beth shakes her head.
"Cigarettes can make you really sick."

206

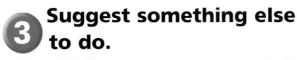

"One cigarette won't hurt you," Sheila says.
"No, thanks. Why don't we go play basketball with Nathan?" Beth asks.

4 Stay with people who also choose healthful activities.

Sheila decides Beth is right and plays basketball with Beth and Nathan.

Problem Solving

Derrel's classmate wants him to drink a beer. Derrel knows that beer contains alcohol and is harmful. Derrel's classmate is trying to make him feel that drinking beer isn't so bad. How can Derrel use the steps for **Refusing** to end this discussion? What decision should Derrel make to show he is trustworthy?

Refusing to Use Alcohol and Tobacco

Lesson Focus

There are ways to help you stay safe from alcohol and tobacco. Plan ahead by thinking of ways to say *no*.

Why Learn This?

Avoiding alcohol and tobacco is an important skill that will help protect your health and safety.

Quick Activity

Saying *Yes* to Good Health List five things you like to do that don't involve using alcohol or tobacco.

Staying Safe from Alcohol and Tobacco

Some of your friends might pressure you to smoke or drink. Many people try alcohol and tobacco when they are young. Some people use alcohol and tobacco because ads make using them look like fun. Others think it will make them look grown up, even though most adults don't use these drugs. Still others try them because friends urge them to. To stay safe from alcohol and tobacco, find friends who don't use these products.

COMPARE AND CONTRAST Compare and contrast the reasons some people try alcohol and tobacco with the truth about these drugs.

Singing

Reading

▲ There are many things to do that don't involve tobacco or alcohol use.

Exercising

208

Ways to Say *No* to Alcohol and Tobacco

It's important to know ahead of time how you can say *no* to alcohol and tobacco use. Then you'll be ready if someone asks you to try them.

Painting

Gardening

Writing

Here are ideas you might try:

- Say *no* and walk away.
- Look surprised and say, "That's against the law."
- Say, "I've promised my parents not to do that."
- Laugh and say, "I want to have fun, not hurt my body."
- Look at a clock. Say, "I have to get going."

With your family or a friend, practice ways to say *no*. Try different ways. Choose the ways you are most comfortable with. Remember, when you say *no*, you might be saving your health—or your life!

Consumer Activity

Analyze Ads and Media Messages Many ads use tricks to sell a product. Being able to identify these tricks can help you plan ways to refuse alcohol and tobacco. Find an ad for alcohol or tobacco. Figure out a trick being used in the ad, and write a way to refuse the product.

Focus Skill **MAIN IDEA AND DETAILS List three ways to refuse alcohol or tobacco.**

Building Good Character

Citizenship Many people in Ed's apartment building are smokers. Ed and his brother sometimes want to play in the building's game room. Often people are smoking there. What could Ed and his brother do to be good citizens and help other people give up unhealthful habits?

No Smoking

Laws About the Use of Alcohol and Tobacco

It's against the law for young people to buy or use alcohol and tobacco. People must be at least 21 years old to buy alcohol. In most states, people under the age of 18 can't buy tobacco.

Laws protect people from the harmful effects of ETS. Most government buildings are smoke-free. In some places, it's against the law to smoke in restaurants and offices.

The government requires labels on alcohol and tobacco products that tell about their dangers. The labels may help people avoid the dangers.

SUMMARIZE How does the government protect people from ETS?

Lesson 3 Summary and Review

❶ **Summarize with Vocabulary**

Use terms from this lesson to complete these statements.

If somebody offers you alcohol or a cigarette, you should say _____. The government requires _____ on alcohol and tobacco products.

❷ List five reasons to avoid alcohol and tobacco.

❸ **Critical Thinking** How can you avoid social situations where people want you to use alcohol and tobacco?

❹ (Focus Skill) **MAIN IDEA AND DETAILS** Draw and complete this graphic organizer to show ways to say *no* to alcohol and tobacco.

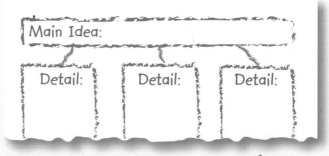

Main Idea:

Detail: | Detail: | Detail:

❺ **Write to Inform—Narration**

Write a story about a young person who is offered cigarettes. Explain how the person shows self-control and refuses the offer.

ACTIVITIES

Science

Body Parts Skit Put on a skit. Have people in the skit play different body parts affected by tobacco and alcohol. Each character can explain how alcohol and tobacco affect the body part.

Home & Community

Communicating Find out what laws your local government has about alcohol. Make a poster showing these laws. Display the poster in a place where people in your community can see it.

Physical Education

An Exercise Plan Some people use exercise as a way of avoiding harmful behaviors like smoking and drinking. Design an exercise program that can be part of a healthful lifestyle.

Career Link

Respiratory Therapist
Respiratory therapists are health-care workers. They help people who have breathing problems and lung diseases. Suppose you are a respiratory therapist. Write a discussion that you and someone who has lung disease might have about the dangers of smoking.

Technology Project

With an adult's help, videotape some classmates acting out ways to refuse tobacco and alcohol. Show your tape to other classes. If you cannot videotape the play, just act it out for an audience.

GO ONLINE For more activities, visit The Learning Site.
www.harcourtschool.com/health

211

About Yourself and Others

Reading Skill

IDENTIFY CAUSE AND EFFECT An effect is something that happens. A cause is the reason, or why, it happens. Use the Reading in Health Handbook on pages 286–287 to help you learn new health facts and ideas in this chapter.

Identify Cause and Effect

Cause:		Effect:

Health Graph

INTERPRET DATA A children's magazine asked its readers what they looked for in a friend. What did the readers want most in a friend?

What Makes a Friend?

Bar graph titled "What Makes a Friend?" with y-axis "Number of Readers" ranging 0 to 100 and x-axis "Character Traits": Funny ≈ 84, Honest ≈ 75, Thoughtful ≈ 86, Caring ≈ 86.

Daily Physical Activity

Being physically active can help you feel good about yourself.

Be Active!
Use the selection **Track 10**, **Super Stress Buster**, to relax you and give your mood a boost.

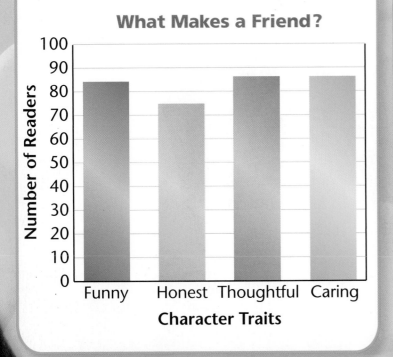

LESSON 1

Understanding Your Feelings

Lesson Focus

When you feel good about yourself, you treat yourself like a friend. You control your feelings and choose how to express those feelings.

Why Learn This?

When you feel good about yourself and control your feelings, it is easier to be happy and get along with others.

Vocabulary

feelings
need
want
body language
emotions
self-control

Feeling good about yourself gives you the courage to try new things. ▶

Feeling Good About Yourself

Everyone has feelings. **Feelings** are the way we react to other people and to the things that happen around us. You might have different feelings about something than others might. For example, you might feel excited about going to a new school. But someone else might feel worried about making new friends at a new school.

Feelings are not good or bad. However, feelings can control you if you do not know what to do with them. Learning about your feelings can help you control them.

How you feel about yourself is important. Treat yourself the same way you would treat a good friend. Being a friend to yourself means respecting yourself. When you *respect* (rih•SPEKT) yourself, you stand up for your ideas. You take good care of yourself.

Being a friend to yourself also means being *responsible* (rih•SPAHN•suh•buhl). When you are responsible, people can count on you. You do what you are supposed to do. Part of being responsible also means being honest.

 CAUSE AND EFFECT **What is an effect of letting angry feelings get out of control?**

Quick Activity

Identify Events List all the events that are influencing this girl's feelings.

217

Ways to Control Feelings

Myth and Fact

Myth: **If you feel anger, you are a bad person.**

Fact: Feeling angry is natural. Having self-control over your anger is what is important.

Everyone has **emotions** (ih•MOH•shuhnz), or strong feelings. The emotions of love and joy may make people happy. However, feelings of sadness and anger make people uncomfortable.

When you have **self-control**, you have power over your emotions. Self-control lets you deal with uncomfortable feelings. You can choose how to express the feelings, or you can let them go.

The first step in self-control is finding the best word to describe your feeling. For example, you might think you are sad, but you might really be lonely. First, name your feeling. Then you can choose how to deal with it.

◀ Sometimes being a positive influence can calm you down.

How can you deal with uncomfortable feelings? Sometimes they go away quickly. If the feelings last for a while, you might need to tell a parent how you feel.

Talking is one way to let anger and other uncomfortable feelings go. Exercise is another way. Sometimes it helps to write about the feeling in a journal. Find the way that works best for you.

SEQUENCE **What is the first step in self-control?**

Personal Health Plan

Real-Life Situation
Sometimes things may make you angry.
Real-Life Plan
List three ways you can control your anger.

More Ways to Control Your Feelings

- Write about your feelings.
- Forgive yourself for making a mistake.
- Forgive others for hurting your feelings.
- Call a friend and do something fun together.
- Read a book that makes you laugh.

If you sor
you need to
need to **ap**
ask the othe
someone ap
This shows

Another
compassion
feel what o
caring way.
are a good

DRAW C
apologi

Lesson 1 Summary and Review

❶ **Summarize with Vocabulary**
Use the vocabulary from this lesson to complete these sentences.

Anger and joy are both _____.
Something that you must have to live is a _____. Something you would like to have is a _____. Strong feelings are called _____. Your feelings show in your words, actions, and _____. You can use _____ to deal with your feelings.

❷ Identify three ways someone can express feelings through body language.

❸ **Critical Thinking** How can you be a good friend to yourself?

❹ (Focus Skill) **CAUSE AND EFFECT** Draw and complete this graphic organizer. In the empty box, name an effect of controlling your feelings.

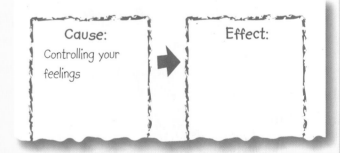

Cause: Controlling your feelings → Effect:

❺ **Write to Express—Friendly Letter**
A friend is feeling sad. Write a friendly letter. Tell your friend some ways to control and express how he or she feels.

221

Listening well does not mean that you just sit quietly. It also means that you say things to show you understand the speaker. Here are the kinds of things someone who listens well might say:

"What happened then?"

"That must have been scary!"

"What will you do now?"

Someone who listens well also uses body language. A good listener looks the speaker in the eye. A listener does not watch television or people walking by. Your words and actions show that you are a kind and respectful listener.

SUMMARIZE What is an example of how to listen with kindness or respect?

▼ Listening is a way to show kindness and respect.

Lesson Focus

Everyone can learn ho[w] to improve listening a[nd] communication skills.

Why Learn Thi[s]

Communicating respectfully helps you better understand an[d] get along with others.

Vocabulary

communicate
apologize
compassion

Health & Techno[logy]

Special Delivery TTY (Text Telephone Yoke) helps people who can[not] hear use telephones. T[he] person who cannot he[ar] types a message into a special machine. After the message has been received a text messag[e] sent back. Then the person is able to read response.

Lesson 4 Summary and Review

❶ Summarize with Vocabulary

Use vocabulary and other terms from this lesson to complete these sentences.

When you share information, you _____. Sharing means both speaking and _____. When you feel what someone else feels, you have _____. When you are wrong, it's best to _____.

❷ Why is listening an important part of communication?

❸ Critical Thinking Why might someone's body language and words not match?

❹ (Focus Skill) CAUSE AND EFFECT Draw and complete this graphic organizer to show how listening well can affect communication.

Cause:		Effect:
Listening well	→	

❺ Write to Express—New Idea

Write a letter to your classmates, listing three reasons you think that everyone should learn to communicate better.

ACTIVITIES

Language Arts

Ways to Get Attention Babies can only cry to get attention. List appropriate ways to get attention at school and at home. How are your two lists the same? How are they different?

Science

Pets Have Feelings, Too Do you have a pet? If not, ask some of your classmates about their pets. Can you observe pets' feelings? How can the owner tell when his or her pet is happy, sad, hungry, or angry? Share your observations with the class.

Technology Project

Use e-mail to let someone know you are thinking about him or her. Tell this friend the most important thing you have learned in this chapter about friends and feelings.

For more activities, visit The Learning Site.
www.harcourtschool.com/health

Home & Community

Sharing Feelings Try this for a week. At dinnertime, have each family member tell how he or she is feeling right then and explain why. You might learn some interesting things about one another! Make sure you are a good listener when others are speaking.

Career Link

Translator for the Deaf
Translators use their fingers and hands to communicate ideas to people who cannot hear. Suppose that you are explaining something for someone who cannot hear. Use body language to help communicate these "I" messages: "I feel sad when people tease me." "I feel happy because I have done well in school."

Reading Skill

IDENTIFY CAUSE AND EFFECT

Draw and use this graphic organizer to answer questions 1 and 2.

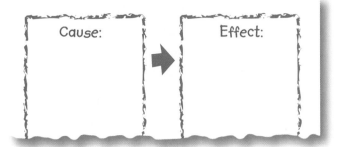

Cause: → Effect:

1 Write one effect of anger.

2 Write one cause of stress.

Use Vocabulary

Match each term in Column B with its meaning in Column A.

Column A	Column B
3 People your own age	**A** want
	B stress
4 To say you are sorry	**C** communicate
	D need
5 Something you must have to live	**E** peers
	F apologize
6 Mental or emotional pressure you feel	
7 Something you would like to have	
8 To share information	

Check Understanding

Choose the letter of the correct answer.

9 Strong feelings are called _____. (p. 220)

  A grief   **C** needs

  B emotions   **D** wants

10 How is this boy showing his feelings? (p. 219)

  F self-control   **H** words

  G body language   **J** anger

11 Some classmates ask you to play a mean trick on someone. This is an example of _____. (p. 230)

  A peer pressure   **C** self-control

  B body language   **D** emotions

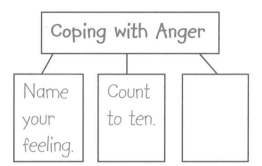

Coping with Anger

| Name your feeling. | Count to ten. | |

12 Which action belongs in the empty box? (p. 224)

 F Take long, slow breaths.

 G Set goals you can reach.

 H Manage your time.

 J Blame the other person.

13 Grief and stress are two _____. (pp. 222–225)

 A needs

 B wants

 C emotions

 D relationships

14 Worry that keeps you awake at night could be a sign of _____. (p. 222)

 F anger **H** fear

 G feelings **J** self-control

15 The way you get along with someone is called a _____. (p. 228)

 A want **C** feeling

 B need **D** relationship

16 Paul does not want anyone to know that he is angry. When his friends ask him what is wrong, he says, "I'm okay." How can his friends tell that Paul is angry?

17 When should you ask a parent or another trusted adult for help with uncomfortable feelings?

18 **BUILDING GOOD CHARACTER**
 Caring You told Sonia that you would meet her at the park on the corner. Now some other friends want you to ride bikes with them. How can you show that you are a good friend?

19 **LIFE SKILLS**
 Manage Stress You are playing softball, and the score is tied. It's your turn at bat. Your legs feel like rubber. How can you cope?

20 **Write to Express—Idea** Give two reasons why it's important to control your feelings.

Reading Skill

SUMMARIZE A summary is a short statement that includes the main idea and the most important details in a passage. Use the Reading in Health Handbook on pages 292–293 and this graphic organizer to help you read the health facts in this chapter.

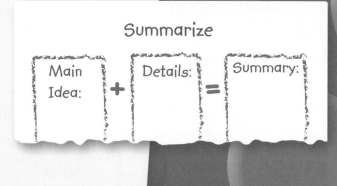

Summarize

| Main Idea: | + | Details: | = | Summary: |

Health Graph

INTERPRET DATA What percentage of families have grandparents living with them? What percentage of families have a grandparent as the head of the family?

Grandparents Living with Families

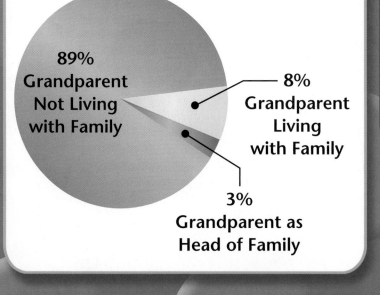

89% Grandparent Not Living with Family

8% Grandparent Living with Family

3% Grandparent as Head of Family

Daily Physical Activity

Exercising with your family can be fun and healthful.

 **Be Active!**
Use the selection **Track 11**, **Funky Flex**, to practice exercises you can share with your family.

Learning About Families

Understanding Families

Not all families are the same. Some families are quiet. Others are noisy. Some are big, and others are small. Many children live with their mother and father. Others live with one parent or have a stepparent. Some children live with a grandparent.

Families love each other in good times and bad times. They help each other when they are sick or scared. They give their children food, a place to sleep, and clothes to wear. Families try hard to give their children what they need to grow up healthy and happy.

 SUMMARIZE **What are ways family members show they care for one another?**

Did You Know?

The fourth Monday of September is Family Day. Family Day is a special day to remind families to eat dinner together. Eating meals together can make families healthier and happier.

Family members find many ways to make their home happy. ▼

▲ When family members are not near, you can write to tell them what you are doing.

Ways Families Communicate

The way that family members talk to each other, or *communicate*, shows how they feel about each other. Choosing appropriate ways to gain attention, such as communicating, shows respect. *Teasing*, or making fun of someone, isn't a good way to get attention and can cause hurt feelings.

Listening is important. Pay attention to the person who is talking. A good listener does not interrupt someone who is talking.

Learn to talk and listen respectfully to all the members of your family. Some families spend time talking during meals. If family members speak politely to one another, everyone is happier. Each family member feels respected.

DRAW CONCLUSIONS **What can happen if family members do not talk respectfully to each other?**

Quick Activity

Communicate with Family Members Sometimes busy family members communicate by writing a note or an e-mail. Write a note or an e-mail to tell a family member about your day.

243

Helping the children in a family learn new things is a value. ▼

Families Are Important

Values are strong beliefs and actions that are important to a family. Spending time together can be an important value. Other values include learning about right and wrong, keeping promises, and being honest. Your family helps you learn these and other values.

Rituals (RICH•oo•uhlz) are activities that have special meaning. They help families grow strong. Families share these activities over and over again. Celebrations often include rituals. Summer vacations and a parent reading you a bedtime story each night are also rituals. Families enjoy their rituals.

MAIN IDEA AND DETAILS What can a family do to become strong?

Lesson 1 Summary and Review

1 Summarize with Vocabulary

Use vocabulary and other terms from this lesson to complete these statements.

A family's strong beliefs and actions are its _____. Values and _____ help make a family strong. Being able to _____ respectfully is an important part of being a family member.

2 List some examples of family values.

3 Critical Thinking How does a family member listen respectfully to another family member?

4 (Focus Skill) SUMMARIZE Draw and complete this graphic organizer to show some different types of families.

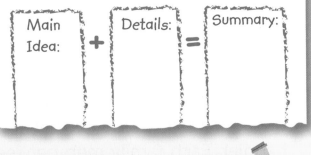

Main Idea: + Details: = Summary:

5 Write to Inform—Description

Write a description of some rituals a family might have.

Fairness

Not Taking Advantage of Others

Family members help each other. Adults do the most difficult jobs, but children can help with many chores. Your older brother might mow the lawn. You might set the table for dinner. Sharing family responsibilities is fair to everyone. Someone who does not do his or her fair share is taking advantage of the other family members.

Family members also are fair to each other when they follow family rules. By sharing the family computer and telephone, for example, you show that you understand each other's needs.

When family members treat each other fairly, they also trust each other. When trust is a value, families feel safe with and close to each other.

- **You are being fair if you think about how what you do affects others.**

- **You are being fair if you treat people the way you want to be treated.**

Activity

Juan needs to be at the bus stop in 30 minutes. Juan has been waiting patiently while Nina is in the bathroom drying her hair. With a partner, role-play what Nina can do to be fair to Juan. How can Nina avoid taking advantage of Juan's patience?

Changes in Families

Lesson Focus

Change can be hard on families.

Why Learn This?

Understanding what change is like can make it less scary.

Vocabulary

sibling
divorce

Ways Families Change

Change happens in families all the time. It often is hard. Even easy changes may have hard parts. Getting a new pet is fun, but there's new work to do. Your pet will need to be fed, cared for, and trained.

Whenever anyone joins or leaves a family, the whole family is affected. A new baby is a huge change in a family. A **sibling** is a brother or a sister. If the new baby is your first sibling, many things will feel different. You might feel happy to have a brother or sister. But you also may not like how much time your parents spend with the baby.

◄ A new baby can cause changes for the whole family.

◀ Having someone move into your home is a big change.

▼ Some families have no children. How many children are in the smallest group of families shown in the graph?

When parents **divorce**, they are no longer married to each other. When a parent gets married again, you have a stepparent. You might have stepsisters and stepbrothers. Divorce and remarriage are big changes.

Other kinds of changes are hard on families. Having an older sibling go away to school can be hard. Moving because of a parent's new job can also be difficult.

⭐ (Focus Skill) **SUMMARIZE** What are some changes that can happen in a family?

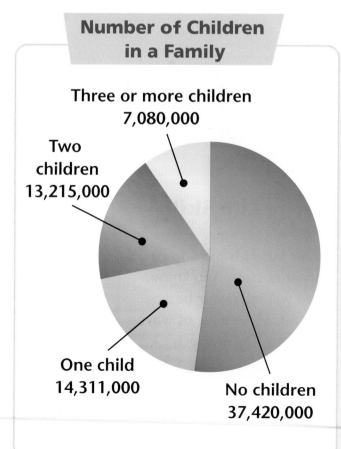

Number of Children in a Family

Three or more children
7,080,000

Two children
13,215,000

One child
14,311,000

No children
37,420,000

247

Quick Activity

Identify Changes

Your grandfather is coming to live with your family. You're looking forward to spending more time with him. But you will now have to share your room with your sibling. List three things that you can do to cope with this change.

▲ New people in your family can mean more fun—and more people to love you.

ACTIVITY

Life Skills

Manage Stress

Your family is moving to another state. You know you will miss your best friend. Make a list of ways you can stay in touch.

Ways to Cope with Changes

What happens if your family changes? Change causes a lot of different feelings. You might wonder how this could happen to you. Whether a change is big or small, family members need time to get used to changes. Feeling angry, sad, afraid, confused—or even just plain weird—is okay.

You can help yourself cope with change. Spending time with your family is very important. Focus on the good things about the change. Try not to reject changes just because they are new or different.

When a change happens in your family, try to be patient with yourself and with other family members. Everyone in your family has feelings about the change. Talk about how you feel, and listen to how others feel. If you have questions, ask them. Finding out what to expect makes going through change easier.

Remember that your whole family is going through the change. Everyone needs time to get used to it. If you need help with a change, talk with a parent or another trusted adult.

SEQUENCE What can you do to cope with a change you know is going to happen?

Lesson 2 Summary and Review

❶ Summarize with Vocabulary

Use vocabulary and other terms from this lesson to complete these statements.

One of the _____ that can happen in a family is _____, or when parents are no longer married to each other. Another change is getting a new _____, or brother or sister. Changes like these can cause a lot of different _____.

❷ What are some changes that can happen in a family when parents divorce?

❸ Critical Thinking In what ways can people in a family be affected by change?

❹ (Focus Skill) **SUMMARIZE** Draw and complete this graphic organizer to show some feelings a new sibling can cause.

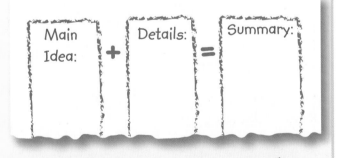

| Main Idea: | + | Details: | = | Summary: |

❺ Write to Inform—Description
Suppose your mother has just remarried. You have moved into your stepfather's home. Write a letter to a friend about your new home.

Resolving Conflicts
By Listening to Others

Listening to family members helps you understand their feelings. Doing this also shows that you care. Using the steps for **Resolving Conflicts** is a way to do that.

Mike and Trisha's parents are ordering out for dinner. Mike and Trisha each want different foods. How can they solve the conflict?

1 Use "I" messages to tell how you feel.

"I never get a chance to choose what we eat," says Mike. "I want Chinese food tonight."

2 Listen to each other.

"We had Chinese last time," says Trisha. "I'm tired of Chinese food. I want something different. I want pizza!"

3 **Negotiate.**

Mike says, "I have an idea. We could take turns. This time, Trisha can pick the food. And next time I'll pick."

4 **Compromise on a solution.**

Everyone is happy with the solution.

 # Problem Solving

Katie has just received a new sweater for her birthday. Her sister Lauren wants to wear Katie's sweater to a friend's party. Katie hasn't had a chance to wear the sweater yet. She doesn't want Lauren to wear it first.

Use the steps for **Resolving Conflicts** to help Katie and Lauren resolve their problem fairly. Be sure both girls demonstrate respect by listening carefully.

Families Help Each Other

Ways Families Work Together

When everyone in a family works together, jobs get done faster. When family members help each other, everyone feels good.

In some families, children have certain jobs. These jobs are their responsibilities. **Responsibilities** are things that someone expects you to do. In some families, one child might always set the table or take care of a pet. In other families, children take turns doing jobs.

DRAW CONCLUSIONS How is sharing the work in a family helpful?

Quick Activity

Working Together
List the different jobs in your family. Next to each job, write who does it.

Chore Chart

	Sunday	Monday	Tuesday	Wednesday	Thursday	Friday
Water the plants	☺	☺	☺			
Feed the bird	☺	☺				
Take out the garbage	☺	☺	☺			
Clean my room	☺	☺				

Roles of a Family Member

Everyone in a family has a part, or **role**, to play. Parents have an adult role. When you were younger, your family did everything for you. Now that you are older, you can help your family.

In your new role, you have new responsibilities. You might help out by reading stories to a younger sibling. A good way to show responsibility is to do a job without waiting to be asked.

Working together can be fun. But each family member has to do his or her part. When everyone acts responsibly, the family can meet all of its members' needs.

COMPARE AND CONTRAST What is the difference between a role and a responsibility?

▲ As you get older, your role changes. You get new responsibilities.

ACTIVITY

Building Good Character

Responsibility Suppose one of your jobs is setting the table for dinner. However, you want to start reading your new book. It will be dinner time in half an hour. Use what you've learned about responsibility to tell what you should do first.

253

Ways Families Have Fun

Family members can have fun together in a lot of ways. Some families like to watch or play sports. Some like to read to each other or go to community events. Most communities have activities for families.

When family members play together, they talk and listen to each other. They get to know each other better. They talk about their feelings. They learn to respect each other. When family members have fun together, they feel close to each other. Feeling close helps a family be happy and healthy.

CAUSE AND EFFECT **What happens when family members have fun together?**

Having fun together is just as important as working together. ▶

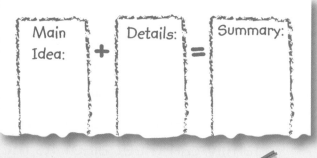

Lesson 3 Summary and Review

❶ Summarize with Vocabulary

Use vocabulary from this lesson to complete these statements.

As children get older, their _____, or the parts they play in the family, change. This means that they have more _____, or things that they are expected to do.

❷ How does having roles help a family?

❸ Critical Thinking How can you be a responsible family member?

❹ (Focus Skill) SUMMARIZE Draw and complete this graphic organizer to show what a family can do to be happy and healthy.

| Main Idea: | + | Details: | = | Summary: |

❺ Write to Inform—Explanation

Write a paragraph about how working and playing together can help a family.

254

ACTIVITIES

Physical Education

Plan an Activity Write an invitation to your family to watch or participate in an athletic or sporting activity. Describe the activity, tell where and when it will take place, and list what everyone needs to bring and wear.

Science

Graph Genetic Traits Many of your physical traits are inherited from your family. Tongue-rolling, dimples, and attached or unattached ear lobes are inherited. Find out how many members of the class have these traits. Then make a graph showing these traits in the class.

Technology Project

Use a computer to research and make a slide show about family life in another country. Describe how families in that country live, work, and play. Present your slide show to your family or classmates. If a computer isn't available, use library books.

 For more activities, visit The Learning Site.
www.harcourtschool.com/health

Home & Community

Communicating Create an ad about things that families can do in your community. Ask parents or other trusted adults how to find out more about community activities.

Career Link

Neonatal Nurse The job of a neonatal nurse is to care for newborn babies. Parents have lots of responsibilities when they arrive home with a new baby. Suppose you are a nurse, helping the parents of a newborn get ready to take their baby home. Make a list of the important things the family needs to know before the baby is taken home.

Chapter Review and Test Preparation

Focus **Reading Skill**

SUMMARIZE

Draw and then use this graphic organizer to answer questions 1 and 2.

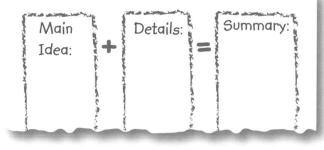

1 What are some kinds of changes that happen to a family?

2 What are some ways to cope with changes that happen in a family?

Use Vocabulary

Match each term in Column B with its meaning in Column A.

Column A	Column B
3 A family's strong beliefs	A divorce
4 A brother or a sister	B responsibilities
5 The part you play in your family	C role
6 The things you are expected to do	D sibling
7 The ending of a marriage	E values

Check Understanding

Choose the letter of the correct answer.

8 Telling the truth is an example of a _____. (p. 244)

A ritual **C** listening skill
B family value **D** family activity

9 When you are listening to someone, it is important to look at him or her and _____. (p. 243)

F to pay attention to what else is going on in the room
G to let the person know if he or she has said something wrong
H to not interrupt what he or she is saying
J to raise your hand before you interrupt

10 When there's a big change in your family, it's normal for you to feel _____. (p. 248)

A sad **C** angry
B excited **D** any of these

11 If a change happens in your family, it is important for you to _____. (p. 249)

F not ask questions
G not go along with the change
H blame someone for the change
J talk about your feelings

12 A new sibling is an example of a family _____. (p. 246)

A change **C** ritual
B chore **D** value

13 Which of the following children is doing his or her responsibility? (p. 252)

F

H

G

J

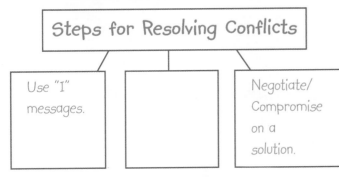

Steps for Resolving Conflicts

Use "I" messages.

Negotiate/ Compromise on a solution.

14 What is missing from the steps for Resolving Conflicts shown in the graphic organizer above? (p. 250)
A Try to get your own way first.
B Keep your feelings to yourself.
C Listen to each other.
D Make a threat.

15 Which of these is a good way to cope with change in a family? (p. 248)
F disagree
G get angry
H focus on good things
J not do chores

16 You have a new baby sister, and she's taking up a lot of your mother's time. What is an appropriate way to gain your mother's attention?

17 You need to finish your homework before dinner. Your older brother has just offered to play ball with you. Explain what you decide to do and why.

Apply Skills

18 **BUILDING GOOD CHARACTER**
Fairness Your older brother said you may play with his favorite toy. How should you take care of the toy while you play with it so that you do not take advantage of your brother?

19 **LIFE SKILLS**
Resolving Conflicts Your new stepbrother has just moved into your house. You find him in your bedroom, and he's just finishing a jigsaw puzzle you've been working on for the last week. You feel upset. How can you resolve this problem by using the steps for Resolving Conflicts?

Write About Health

20 **Write to Inform—Explanation**
Explain what a family can do to be happy and healthy.

CHAPTER 12 Health in the Community

Our Community Helpers

Reading Skill

COMPARE AND CONTRAST When you compare, you tell how two or more things are alike. When you contrast, you tell how they are different. Use the Reading in Health Handbook on pages 282–283 and this graphic organizer to help you read the health facts in this chapter.

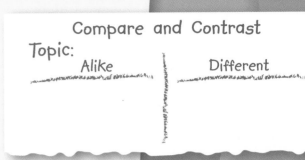

Compare and Contrast
Topic:
Alike   Different

Health Graph

INTERPRET DATA Many people are needed to serve in health jobs. How can you explain the increase in the number of people in health jobs over the 30 years shown on the graph?

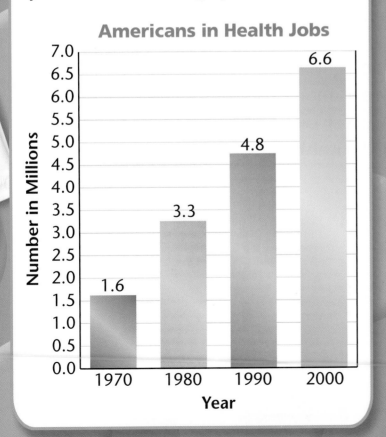

Americans in Health Jobs

Number in Millions

1970: 1.6
1980: 3.3
1990: 4.8
2000: 6.6

Year

Daily Physical Activity

There are many ways and places to get physically involved in your community.

Be Active!
Use the selection **Track 12, Broadway Bound**, to share some exercise time with your classroom community.

Where to Get Health Care

Lesson Focus

Health departments, hospitals, and clinics treat people who are hurt or ill. They help people stay well, too.

Why Learn This?

You can use what you learn to find places in your community to get health care.

Vocabulary

community
health department
hospital
clinic
health screenings

Health Departments

A **community** (kuh•MYOO•nuh•tee) is a place where people live, work, play, and go to school. Doctors, nurses, and other health-care workers in your community help you stay healthy. A **health department** is a group of health workers who serve a community. People who work for a health department are also called public health workers.

Public health workers give health care and advice to people in the community. They have offices that you can visit or call if you have a problem. Public health nurses visit and care for people who aren't able to leave home. Some public health nurses give people vaccinations. Many also have websites that you can visit for more information.

COMPARE AND CONTRAST How are some public health nurses the same and different?

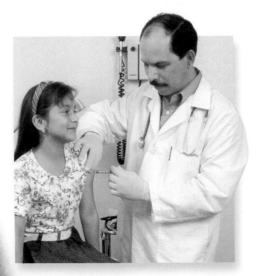

◄ Many women go to a hospital to give birth to their babies. There, doctors, nurses, and midwives can make sure the mothers and babies stay as well as possible.

Hospitals

A **hospital** (HAHS•piht•uhl) is a place where people who are ill or hurt can get medical treatment. In hospitals doctors, nurses, and other workers care for people who cannot get well at home. These people might need a special doctor such as a surgeon. Surgeons are doctors who perform operations. They might repair a person's heart or remove a body part that is diseased.

Some people go to hospitals because they need special medical equipment or medicine to help them get better. Many people who have had bad accidents visit the emergency room in a hospital.

DRAW CONCLUSIONS Where would you most likely have your tonsils removed?

Did You Know?

More than 120,000 children are treated at emergency rooms each year for head injuries from bicycle crashes. Wearing a bike helmet properly can reduce the risk of brain injury.

261

ACTIVITY

Life Skills

Communicate

It is important to tell trusted adults when you aren't feeling well. Suppose your throat began hurting after lunch and continued to feel sore when you got home. What would you do?

Clinics

People who need medical treatment can also go to a **clinic** (KLIN•ik). Most clinics cost less than hospitals. Some are even free. Doctors and nurses in clinics treat people who have minor illnesses or injuries. People who are very ill or badly hurt must go to a hospital.

People can also get regular checkups at a clinic. For example, a doctor or nurse can check your eyes or give you a vaccination. Many clinics also teach people about health and safety. They offer **health screenings**, or tests, that check for diseases.

DRAW CONCLUSIONS Why would someone decide to go to a clinic rather than a hospital?

Quick Activity

Health Screenings
List three ways you can cooperate during a health screening.

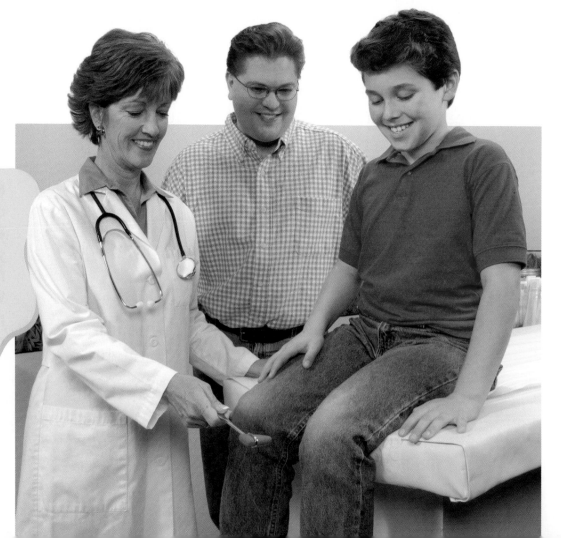

Health-Care Helpers

In addition to doctors and nurses, many other people in your community help keep you healthy and safe. Police officers, firefighters, and paramedics are there to help you if you get hurt. School nurses are also health-care resources. They may give you information about health.

If you need to get in touch with a community helper, you can find phone numbers and addresses in a phone book or on the Internet. You can ask a parent or another trusted adult to help you.

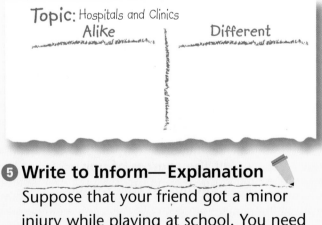

▼ School nurses help keep you safe.

DRAW CONCLUSIONS Demonstrate how you might get in touch with a doctor, school nurse, or other health-care helper.

Lesson 1 Summary and Review

❶ Summarize with Vocabulary
Use vocabulary from this lesson to complete these statements.

A _____ is made up of a group of health-care workers. These workers help people in the _____ stay healthy and safe. You should go to a _____ for serious illnesses or injuries.

❷ Name two places in the community where people who are ill or hurt can get care.

❸ Critical Thinking Why is it important to cooperate with parents and health-care workers who treat diseases?

❹ COMPARE AND CONTRAST
Draw and complete this graphic organizer to show how a hospital and clinic are alike and different.

Topic: Hospitals and Clinics

Alike	Different

❺ Write to Inform—Explanation
Suppose that your friend got a minor injury while playing at school. You need to get some help for him or her. List who at your school you could go to for help. Explain why you chose that person.

Keeping the Environment Healthful

Lesson Focus

Clean air and protection from noise are important to your health.

Why Learn This?

You can use what you learn to reduce air and noise pollution and to help keep yourself healthy.

Vocabulary

environment
pollution
noise pollution
air pollution
pollution control
  technician

Pollution

Everything around you is part of the **environment** (en•VY•ruhn•muhnt). The environment includes all nonliving things, such as air, water, land, streets, and buildings. It also includes living things, such as plants, animals, and people.

Pollution (puh•LOO•shuhn) is something that makes the environment unhealthful. Smoke in the air is an example of pollution.

CAUSE AND EFFECT What is the effect of pollution?

Quick Activity

Identify Noise Pollution Make a list of the sources of noise pollution in this scene.

Noise Pollution

Disturbing or harmful sounds made by human activities are **noise pollution**. Noise pollution can give you earaches and headaches and can make you tired. It can also make people nervous and cause stress. Many cities have laws against noise pollution.

Sometimes you can avoid noise pollution by moving away from it. Other times the only thing you can do is protect your ears with earplugs.

You can improve your environment by not causing noise pollution. For example, you can turn down the volume of your radio, CD player, and television. You can speak quietly with your family and friends instead of yelling. This will help make your environment a more healthful place to be.

DRAW CONCLUSIONS If you have to shout over your music to be heard by someone else, what does this tell you?

Consumer Activity

Access Valid Health Information Noise is measured by how loud it is. With a parent or family member research the loudness level of at least five different noises. Make a table to share your findings.

Hybrid Cars Hybrid cars run on a combination of gasoline and electricity. The electric battery charges as the car is driven, so it never has to be plugged in. The car can go nearly twice as far on a gallon of gas as a regular car. Hybrid cars save energy and cause less pollution.

Air Pollution

Harmful materials in the air cause **air pollution**. Car exhaust and tobacco smoke are examples of air pollution.

Clean air is important. Air pollution can cause respiratory problems, making it harder to breathe. Many communities have laws to help reduce air pollution. For example, in some states people are not allowed to smoke in public places. Some people have jobs reducing air pollution. A **pollution control technician**, for example, tests water, air, or soil for harmful substances.

DRAW CONCLUSIONS You usually ride in a car when you go to the park. How could you reduce air pollution?

Lesson 2 Summary and Review

❶ Summarize with Vocabulary

Use vocabulary from this lesson to complete these statements.

Everything around us is part of our _____, which can be made unhealthful by _____. Harmful materials in the air are _____. Disturbing or harmful sounds made by human activities are _____. People who test water, air, or soil for harmful substances are called _____.

❷ Give two examples of air pollution.

❸ Critical Thinking What kinds of pollution would you encounter if you lived next to a highway or a train track?

❹ (Focus Skill) COMPARE AND CONTRAST

Draw and complete this graphic organizer about pollution.

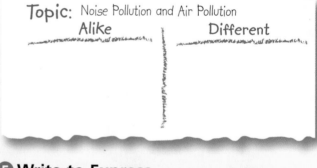

Topic: Noise Pollution and Air Pollution
Alike | Different

❺ Write to Express— Solution to a Problem

Your neighbor plays his stereo very loudly. It disturbs you. He says he can play his music as loud as he wants. What do you think? Write a paragraph explaining how you might solve this problem.

Citizenship

Taking Pride in Your School

You spend a lot of your day at school. It is a special place. Taking pride in your school community is important. Doing so helps make your school a great place to learn. How do you show pride in your school community? Here are some ways to be a good school citizen.

- **Speak respectfully to all members of your school community and to visitors.**
- **Organize a school cleaning day with your peers.**
- **Throw trash in trash bins.**
- **Pick up litter on school grounds.**
- **Decorate the halls with schoolwork and artwork.**
- **Make a school newsletter, or write an article for the existing newsletter.**
- **Have a good attitude.**
- **Make posters reminding people to throw trash in trash bins.**
- **Follow school rules.**

Activity

Before you leave a classroom, take some time to put the classroom in order. Think about the next group that will use the classroom. Before you leave, step back and look at the room. Ask yourself if it looks better than it did before you used it.

267

Controlling Water Pollution

Lesson Focus

Water can become polluted in many ways. Technicians and other people can help control water pollution.

Why Learn This?

You can use what you learn to help protect the water.

Vocabulary

water pollution
groundwater

Keeping Water Clean

Have you ever wondered where wastewater goes after it leaves a sink or a toilet? The used water and other waste are called *sewage*. In most places in the United States, it flows through underground pipes to a sewage treatment plant. There it is treated and made clean and safe to drink and use. If it wasn't treated, the sewage would flow right into rivers, lakes, bays, and oceans. The water would quickly become so polluted that it would be unsafe to drink, swim in, or even touch.

First Stage: The water then goes into a settling tank, where large particles slowly settle out.

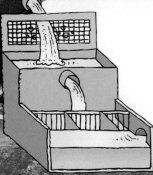

Before Treatment: Wastewater flows through a series of screens. The screens strain out large solid objects, such as pieces of plastic.

Harmful materials such as chemicals and pathogens, or germs, that get in water are **water pollution**. There are many kinds of water pollution.

Sewage in a stream is an example of water pollution. Motor oil dumped into a lake is another example. Water pollution can harm people, animals, and plants.

Some cities get their drinking water from lakes or reservoirs. Water that is to be used for drinking and comes straight from lakes also must be treated. Even if it doesn't look dirty, it can still be polluted. Water picks up pollution when rain falls through polluted air or water flows over polluted land.

SEQUENCE **In the sequence of cleaning sewage water, what happens after particles settle out of the water in settling tanks?**

Second Stage: The water goes into another tank, where bacteria are added to it. These bacteria "eat" many of the wastes still left in the water.

Third Stage: At the last stage, chemicals are added to the water. Some of the chemicals combine with the rest of the pollutants to make them settle out. Chlorine is added to kill bacteria. Then another chemical is added to get rid of the chlorine.

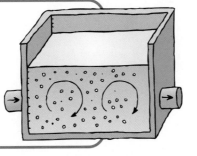

Groundwater Pollution

Where does your drinking water come from? Some comes from large lakes or reservoirs. But more than half of the water that we drink in the United States comes from underground. This water is called **groundwater** . Groundwater sinks into the soil and fills gaps between rocks.

Chemicals from factories, mines, lawns, and farms can also sink into the ground and pollute groundwater. Oil and gasoline from cars, and salt that is used to treat icy roads, can also pollute water under the ground. Paint, lead, fertilizers, and weedkillers can pollute groundwater, too.

MAIN IDEA AND DETAILS Explain how groundwater can get polluted.

▼ Groundwater fills cracks and small spaces in rocks underground. Groundwater comes to the surface through wells and springs.

Stopping Water Pollution

There are things we can do to prevent water pollution. Never dump trash near water. Never remove lead or other toxic substances on your own. If you have leftover paint, motor oil, or other chemicals to get rid of, call your local waste collection department to find out where you can take them. Some people make an entire career out of caring for our water supply.

MAIN IDEA AND DETAILS How can you keep the environment safe from water pollution?

This pollution control technician is testing the water in the river to make sure it is not polluted. ▶

ACTIVITY

Building Good Character

Respect for Others You have finished making a model car, and you want to throw away the leftover glue and paint. Draw a poster that shows what you should do. How does your decision show respect for others?

Lesson 3 Summary and Review

1 Summarize with Vocabulary
Use vocabulary and other terms from this lesson to complete these statements.

After we use water, it must be sent to a _____ to be cleaned. Harmful material in our lakes, oceans, or rivers is called _____. Pollution _____ check water sources for pollution.

2 What happens to most sewage water before it flows into a river or another body of water?

3 Critical Thinking How could pouring paint down the drain harm others?

4 (Focus Skill) COMPARE AND CONTRAST
Draw and complete this graphic organizer.

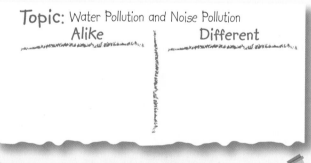

Topic: Water Pollution and Noise Pollution
Alike   Different

5 Write to Express—Business Letter
Write a letter to your local government requesting information about how water pollution is controlled. Your request could ask about special trash pickups of old motor oil, paint, and chemicals or about lead removal.

Set Goals

To Improve Your Community and Environment

You can do things to improve your community and environment. Using the steps for **Setting Goals** can help you make a difference.

Scott's family goes to a lake for a picnic every summer. When they arrived this year, they found a lot of trash. What can Scott do?

1 **Choose a goal.**

Scott wants to clean up the area around the lake.

2 **List and plan steps to meet the goal.**

Scott makes a map of the area that needs to be cleaned and asks his friends to help.

3 Check your progress as you work toward the goal.

Scott and his friends work together to clean up the area. Each of them puts an *X* on the map as they clean each area.

4 Meet your goal, and evaluate the work.

Scott and his friends cleaned up the area. The lake is now a nicer place to be.

Problem Solving

Erica notices trash around the school playground fence. The amount of trash seems to grow each day. Erica notices that someone has moved the trash bin across the street, outside the schoolyard. She is not sure who is responsible for cleaning up the trash or who moved the trash bin.

Use the steps for **Setting Goals** to describe how Erica can solve this problem. Explain what would be the most responsible decision for Erica to make to show respect for her school.

Reduce, Reuse, Recycle

Protect the Environment from Trash

Putting trash in a place that is not a trash can or other proper place is called **littering**. Littering harms plants, animals, and people. Plants covered by litter may not grow well. Animals may mistake litter for food, eat it, and then get sick. Pollution from littering can make humans sick, too.

You can help keep litter from harming your environment by never littering. You can also work with your family and school to stop littering in your community.

SUMMARIZE **List how littering harms plants and animals.**

Myth and Fact

Myth: **Litter isn't unhealthful for people. It's just ugly.**

Fact: Litter provides a place for rats and disease-causing bacteria. It can also provide a place for fire to start. Car crashes are often caused by litter.

Reduce

One way to cut down on littering is to **reduce** the amount of trash you create. Each day, the average person throws away more than 4 pounds of trash. Diseases are sometimes spread from trash dumps.

How can you reduce trash? You could drink water from a glass instead of a paper or plastic cup. You could use a cloth bag when you go shopping instead of using one made of paper or plastic. Less trash means fewer trash dumps. Reducing trash also saves trees and water.

DRAW CONCLUSIONS **About how many pounds of trash does the average person throw away in a week?**

▼ Keeping the beaches litter-free helps animals such as sea turtles. They can lay eggs without mistaking litter for food.

Did You Know?

One-third of all our garbage is the packaging that items come in.

Quick Activity

Analyze Littering
Find another animal that littering can harm. Use reference sources as needed.

275

Reuse

You also protect the environment when you **reuse**, or use something again. When you use something again, you help save Earth's resources.

How can you reuse something? You can pack your lunch in a container that can be reused. You can reuse bags from stores or the comics from the newspaper as wrapping paper. Families can reuse clothing by having older children pass their clothes down to younger children. Community clubs and organizations can set up places where used items can be exchanged. Next time you are going to throw something away, ask yourself whether you or someone else can reuse it.

SUMMARIZE List some ways you can reduce trash through reusing.

How are people in these photos reducing waste through reusing? ▶

Recycle

To **recycle** means to collect used things so they can be made into new things. Glass, metal, paper, and plastic can all be recycled.

Recycling helps cut down on litter in the community. Recycling can also help your community save money. It often takes less energy to make things from recycled material than from new material. Recycling protects important natural resources, too. For example, recycling paper can save trees and reduce air pollution.

SUMMARIZE How does recycling paper preserve nature's resources?

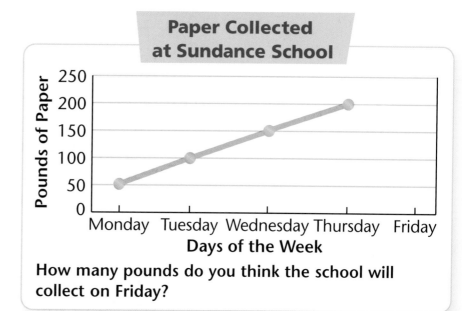

Paper Collected at Sundance School

How many pounds do you think the school will collect on Friday?

Plastics are stamped with a number code. The codes help people at the recycling center sort the plastics. What new products will your recycled plastics make? ▼

Recycling Plastics

Code	Original Objects	New Products
1	soft-drink bottles, peanut butter jars	surfboards, skis, carpets
2	milk and water jugs, margarine cups	trash cans, stadium seats, toys
3	shampoo bottles, clear food-wrap	floor mats, pipes, hoses
4	grocery bags, bread bags	grocery and other types of bags
5	bottle caps, yogurt caps	food trays, car battery parts
6	plastic spoons, meat trays	trash cans, egg cartons, hangers
7	layers of packing materials	plastic lumber

A Healthful Environment

▼ Sea turtle hatchlings take their first steps across a clean beach.

When you reduce, reuse, and recycle, you help protect natural resources that cannot be easily replaced. For example, reusing and recycling paper helps save the trees in our forests. Caring for these resources will help keep the environment healthful.

You can also keep your environment healthful by not littering. Litter can cause disease and make your community look ugly. It can harm the places where animals live, too. You can keep the environment healthful by cleaning up litter in your community.

DRAW CONCLUSIONS What might a healthful community look like?

Lesson 4 Summary and Review

❶ Summarize with Vocabulary

Use vocabulary from this lesson to complete these statements.

We can avoid _____ by putting trash in a trash bin. We should _____, or make less, trash to make our environment more healthful. One way to do this is to _____, or use items again, when we can. We can _____ used paper, plastic, glass, and metal, which can be used to make new products.

❷ What are four ways you can help solve the trash problem?

❸ Critical Thinking If you can drink from a paper cup or glass, which would you choose to help reduce trash?

❹ COMPARE AND CONTRAST

Draw and complete this graphic organizer to show how recycling and reusing are alike and different.

Topic: Reusing and Recycling

Alike | Different

❺ Write to Inform—How-To

Write a plan for how you can help solve the trash problem in your classroom. In your plan, include ways you can reduce, reuse, and recycle.

278

ACTIVITIES

Physical Education

Keep Fit Caring for the environment can help keep your body fit. Picking up trash in your schoolyard gives you exercise. Make a list of some other ways you can keep fit and care for the environment and resources, too.

Science

Airplane
Dogs barking
Radio
Traffic

Noise Pollution
Study the drawing on pages 264–265. List sounds that aren't shown in the drawing. Underline the sounds you think are the loudest. Put a star next to sounds you have heard in the last week. Circle the noises that are hard to get away from. How can you change your own habits to make your surroundings quieter?

Technology Project

Use a digital camera to photograph a littered area in or near your school. Clean up the area with the help of friends and teachers, and then take another photograph. Make a "Before and After" slide presentation with the photographs.

GO ONLINE **For more activities**, visit **The Learning Site.**
www.harcourtschool.com/health

Home & Community

Communicating With family members , locate resources about the kinds of information your health department provides to the public. Make a poster that lists these topics. Use your poster to inform people in your school community about where they can find community health information.

Career Link

Firefighter Firefighters not only put out fires, they do much more. Some teach about fire prevention. Suppose you are a firefighter in your community. You are going to a kindergarten to teach children about safety. Make a script for what you will tell the children. You might want to talk about the fact that litter can cause fires, for example.

Reading Skill

COMPARE AND CONTRAST

Draw and then use this graphic organizer to answer questions 1 and 2.

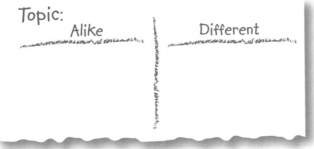

Topic:
Alike — Different

1 How are a clinic and hospital alike and different?

2 How are reusing and recycling alike and different?

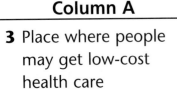 **Use Vocabulary**

Match each term in Column B with its meaning in Column A.

Column A	Column B
3 Place where people may get low-cost health care	**A** pollution
4 Materials in the air that are harmful	**B** noise pollution
5 Place where people live, work, and play	**C** hospital
	D community
	E clinic
6 Place where badly hurt or very sick people get health care	**F** air pollution
7 Disturbing or harmful sounds made by human activities	
8 Harmful materials in the air, water, or land	

Check Understanding

Choose the letter of the correct answer.

9 To make new glass jars from used glass jars, you need to _____ the used glass jars. (p. 277)

A replace   **C** reduce

B reuse   **D** recycle

10 When you give a coat you have outgrown to a younger child, you _____. (p. 276)

F reduce   **H** recycle

G reuse   **J** refuse

11 Which of the following are you doing if you throw trash on the ground? (p. 274)

A reducing   **C** littering

B recycling   **D** reusing

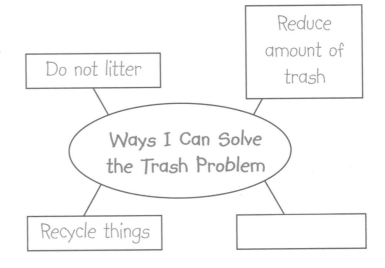

Do not litter

Reduce amount of trash

Ways I Can Solve the Trash Problem

Recycle things

12 Which is missing from the graphic organizer? (p. 278)

F visit hospitals

G health departments

H throw more items away

J reuse materials

13 Which of the following cannot be recycled into a new product you can buy? (p. 277)

A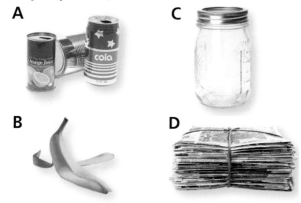

C

B

D

14 A public health worker who tests water, air, or soil for harmful substances is a _____. (p. 266)
 F pollution control technician
 G public health nurse
 H polluter
 J emergency room doctor

15 Harmful material in lakes, oceans, or rivers is _____. (p. 269)
 A air pollution
 B water pollution
 C noise pollution
 D littering

Think Critically

16 If someone has fallen and thinks he or she might have a broken arm, should he or she go to a hospital or to a clinic? Why?

17 How is the job of a school nurse important to your health?

Apply Skills

18 **BUILDING GOOD CHARACTER**
Citizenship You notice that the entrance to your school could be more attractive. Apply what you know about citizenship to describe how to handle the problem.

19 **LIFE SKILLS**
Set Goals You like the convenience of prepackaged individual servings of pretzels. You are now more aware of the extra waste they make. Use what you know about setting goals to describe a change that will contribute to a much more healthful community.

Write About Health

20 **Write to Inform—Explanation**
Explain what steps are taken in your community to provide health information and health services.

Compare and Contrast

Learning how to compare and contrast can help you understand what you read. You can use a graphic organizer like this one to help you compare and contrast what you read.

Topic: Name the topic—the two things you are comparing and contrasting.

Alike	Different
List ways the things are alike.	List ways the things are different.

Tips for Comparing and Contrasting

- To compare, ask—*How are things alike?*
- To contrast, ask—*How are things different?*
- When you compare, look for signal words such as *both*, *too*, and *also*.
- When you contrast, look for signal words such as *different*, *however*, and *but*.

Here is an example.

Compare →

> Pete and Matt eat lunch together every day. Pete is sure to have many healthful foods. Matt is different from Pete. He eats only junk food for his lunch. Pete always has a lot of energy to do his work. Matt *seems* to be tired every afternoon.

← Contrast

Here is what you could record in the graphic organizer.

Topic: Pete and Matt at lunch

Alike	Different
Eat lunch together daily	Pete — healthful food, energy
	Matt — junk food, no energy after lunch

More About Compare and Contrast

You can better understand new information about things when you know how they are alike and how they are different. Use the graphic organizer from page 282 to sort the following new information about Pete and Matt.

Pete	Likes to eat apples	Does not like chips and dip	Loves to eat bananas	Enjoys a diet with variety
Matt	Loves cookies	Enjoys soda with lunch	Likes to eat apples	Loves to eat hot dogs

Sometimes a paragraph compares and contrasts more than one topic. In the following paragraph, one topic is underlined. Find a second topic being compared and contrasted.

Gayle's mom is a nurse. Her dad is a doctor. They both work long hours. Both parents enjoy their jobs. Gayle's mom works at a children's hospital. Gayle's dad works at a clinic. Her parents agree that both places give excellent care.

Skill Practice

Read the following paragraph. Use the Tips for Comparing and Contrasting to answer the questions.

People go to clinics and hospitals when they are hurt or sick. Health-care workers work in both clinics and hospitals to help people get well. Clinics treat people for minor illnesses or injuries. Hospitals are different, because they treat people who are too ill to get well at home.

1 What is one likeness that clinics and hospitals have?

2 What is one difference between clinics and hospitals?

3 What two signal words helped you identify likenesses and differences in this paragraph?

Draw Conclusions

To draw conclusions, use information from the text you are reading and what you already know. Drawing conclusions can help you understand what you read. You can use a graphic organizer like this one to help you draw conclusions.

What I Read		What I Know		Conclusion:
List facts from the text.	+	List related ideas that you already know.	=	Combine what you just read in the text with what you know from before.

Tips for Drawing Conclusions

- To draw conclusions, ask—*What do I need to think about from the text?*
- To draw conclusions, ask—*What do I already know that could help me draw a conclusion?*
- Be sure your conclusion makes sense.

Here is an example.

> Story information
>
> Robbie wanted to buy some paper to make airplanes. Robbie's mom did not want him to walk to the store, because it was too far away. Robbie knew that she set limits because she cared. Robbie asked his mom to drive him to the store. She said that she was busy. Robbie looked over at his dad and smiled.
>
> Your own experience

Here is what you could record in the graphic organizer.

What I Read		What I Know		Conclusion:
Robbie's mom did not want him to walk to the store alone. She could not drive him.	+	When Robbie smiled at his dad, he was trying to get him to give him a ride.	=	Instead of walking to the store, Robbie asked his dad for a ride.

284

More About Drawing Conclusions

Be sure that your conclusions make sense. For example, suppose the paragraph on page 284 included a sentence that said Robbie noticed he had some paper he could use. You could then draw a different conclusion.

What I Read		What I Know		Conclusion:
Robbie's mom did not want him to walk to the store alone. She could not drive him.	+	When a person already has some of what is needed, there is no rush to buy more.	=	Robbie decided he did not need to go to the store after all.

Sometimes a paragraph might not contain enough information to draw a conclusion that makes sense. Read the paragraph below. Think of one right conclusion you could draw. Then think of a conclusion that would be wrong.

A safety rule in Mike's family is that nobody can run into the street. Mike does not like that rule because sometimes his ball rolls away. When Mike's mom was outside one day, his ball rolled right in front of a car. He looked at his mom. She was busy working in her flower bed.

Skill Practice

Read the following paragraph. Use the Tips for Drawing Conclusions to answer the questions.

Dario needed a spray bottle for a school project. He saw one on a high shelf in the garage. The bottle did not look familiar. He thought about the things in the garage that are dangerous. He walked back into the house.

1 What conclusion can you draw about Dario's decision about the spray bottle?

2 What information from your own experience helped you draw the conclusion?

3 What story information did you use to draw the conclusion?

Identify Cause and Effect

Learning how to identify cause and effect can help you understand why things happen. You can use a graphic organizer like this one to show cause and effect.

> Cause:
> A cause is the reason, or why, something happens.

➤

> Effect:
> An effect is what happens.

Tips for Identifying Cause and Effect

- To find an effect, ask—*What happened?*
- To find a cause, ask—*Why did this happen?*
- Remember that events can have more than one cause or effect.
- Look for signal words such as *because*.

Here is an example.

> Cause
>
> Effect

> Amber walked into her new classroom. She was feeling scared. She thought about what her dad said the night before. She knew that soon she would have new friends. Amber started to feel better.

Here is what you could record in the graphic organizer.

> Cause:
> New classroom

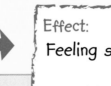

> Effect:
> Feeling scared

More About Cause and Effect

Events can have more than one cause or effect. For example, suppose the paragraph on page 286 included a sentence that said Amber could feel her heart beat faster. You could then identify two effects of Amber's new classroom.

Cause:
New classroom

Effect:
Feeling scared

Effect:
Fast heartbeat

Some paragraphs contain more than one cause and effect. In the following paragraph, one cause and its effect are underlined. Find a second cause and its effect.

Sam loved running around the track with his friends. <u>Running made his pulse go faster.</u> He knew this was good for his heart and lungs. One day, Sam felt a cramp in his leg. He stopped and massaged his muscle. The cramp went away. He knew that he should have had more water to drink.

Skill Practice

Read the following paragraph. Use the Tips for Identifying Cause and Effect to help you answer the questions.

Kristy was excited because her dance recital was in two days. She practiced her dance many times. The night before the show, Kristy practiced hard, but she forgot to stretch her muscles first. She pulled a muscle in her leg. Kristy could not be in the dance recital.

1 What caused Kristy to miss the recital?

2 What was the effect of not stretching her muscles before a practice?

3 Name a signal word that helped you identify a cause or an effect.

⭐ Identify the Main Idea and Details

Being able to identify the main idea and details can help you understand what you read. You can use a graphic organizer like this one to show the main idea and details.

> **Main Idea:** The most important idea of a selection

> **Detail:** More information about the main idea

> **Detail:** More information about the main idea

> **Detail:** More information about the main idea

Tips for Identifying the Main Idea and Details

- To find the main idea, ask—*What is this mostly about?*
- Remember that the main idea is not always stated in the first sentence.
- Be sure to look for details that help you answer questions such as *who*, *what*, *where*, and *when*.
- Use pictures as clues to help you figure out the main idea.

Here is an example.

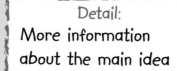

> Main Idea

> The bones in your head make up your skull. Some of the bones protect your brain. Others protect your eyes. The bones in your face are part of your skull, too.

> Detail

Here is what you could record in the graphic organizer.

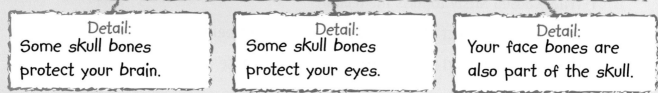

> **Main Idea:** The bones in your head make up your skull.

> **Detail:** Some skull bones protect your brain.

> **Detail:** Some skull bones protect your eyes.

> **Detail:** Your face bones are also part of the skull.

More About Main Idea and Details

Sometimes the main idea of a paragraph is at the end instead of the beginning. If the main idea is not given at all, look at the details to figure it out. Look at the graphic organizer. What do you think the main idea is?

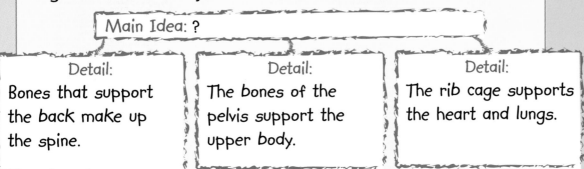

Main Idea: ?

Detail:
Bones that support the back make up the spine.

Detail:
The bones of the pelvis support the upper body.

Detail:
The rib cage supports the heart and lungs.

Sometimes a paragraph's main idea contains details of different types. In the following paragraph, identify whether the details give reasons, examples, facts, steps, or descriptions.

Bones protect parts of your body, so it is important to protect your bones. Calcium helps bones grow and makes them strong. Exercise also makes your bones strong. Not caring for bones can make them break easily.

Skill Practice

Read the following paragraph. Use the Tips for Identifying the Main Idea and Details to answer the questions.

Tobacco smoke can harm a person's body. The smoke has more than 4,000 things in it. One of those is tar. Tar makes breathing hard. Tobacco smoke can also cause people to cough. People who smoke tobacco may die from lung cancer or other lung diseases.

1 What is the main idea of the paragraph?

2 What details give more information about the main idea?

3 What details answer any of the questions *who, what, where,* and *when*?

Sequence

Paying attention to the sequence of events, or the order in which things happen, can help you understand what you read. You can use a graphic organizer like this one to show sequence.

| 1. The first thing that happened | → | 2. The next thing that happened | → | 3. The last thing that happened |

Tips for Understanding Sequence

- Pay attention to the order in which events happen.
- Recall dates and times to help you understand the sequence.
- Look for time-order signal words such as *first*, *next*, *then*, *last*, and *finally*.
- Sometimes it is helpful to add time-order words yourself as you read.

Here is an example.

Time-order word →

Beth's dad could tell that Beth was not feeling well. First, she did not eat much of her supper. Then, Beth said that her head and throat hurt. Finally, Beth's dad took her temperature. Sure enough, Beth was sick.

← Time-order word

Here is what you could record in the graphic organizer.

| 1. Beth did not eat her supper. | → | 2. Beth said her throat and head hurt. | → | 3. Dad found out that she had a fever. |

More About Sequence

Sometimes information is sequenced by dates. For example, do you remember when you got vaccines for some diseases? Use a graphic organizer like the following to sequence the order in which you got your shots.

1. Hepatitis B: March 12, 2002  2. Measles, mumps, rubella: June 11, 2002 → 3. Chicken pox: September 13, 2002

When time-order words are not given, add your own. Look at the underlined time-order word in the paragraph below. How many more time-order words can you add to help you understand the sequence?

When you exercise, remember to warm up and cool down. <u>First</u>, warm up by stretching your muscles. This may take a few minutes. Do your main exercises. Spend a few minutes doing an easier activity to cool down.

Skill Practice

Read the following paragraph. Use the Tips for Understanding Sequence to answer the questions.

If you hear a smoke alarm beep, you may need to escape a fire. First, drop down and stay low. Crawl away quickly. Next, warn others. Shout or blow a whistle if you can. Then, follow an escape path. Open a closed door only if it is cool. Last, after you get to your family's meeting place, call 911 or the fire department.

1 What are the first things you should do to escape a fire?

2 What might happen if you do not follow the right sequence or leave out a step when escaping a fire?

3 What four signal words helped you identify the sequence in this paragraph?

⭐ Focus Skill Summarize

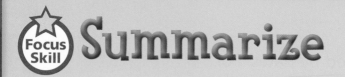

Learning how to summarize helps you use your own words to tell what something is about. This can help you understand what you read. You can use a graphic organizer like this one to summarize.

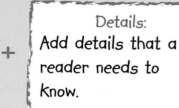

Main Idea:		Details:		Summary:
Tell about the most important things that happened.	+	Add details that a reader needs to know.	=	Retell what you have just read. Use the main idea and only the most important details.

Tips for Summarizing

- To write a summary, ask—*What is the most important idea or the main thing that happened?*
- Be sure the details you include are things the reader needs to know.
- Make your summary shorter than what you have read.
- Write a summary in your own words. Be sure to put the events in order.

Here is an example.

Main Idea   Details

   Family members are a big part of your life. They want you to be responsible. They want you to have fun and play fair. When your family has problems, all of you should work together. Your family gives you care and support.

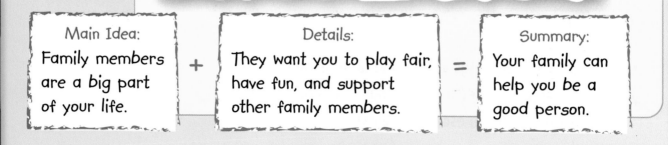

Main Idea:		Details:		Summary:
Family members are a big part of your life.	+	They want you to play fair, have fun, and support other family members.	=	Your family can help you *be a* good person.

More About Summarizing

Sometimes a paragraph has details that are not important enough to put in a summary. What if the paragraph on page 292 included a sentence about jobs to do around the house? You would leave that detail out of the summary. It would not be important to understanding the main idea.

Main Idea:		Details:		Summary:
Your family is a big part of your life.	+	They expect you to behave in a certain way.	=	Your family helps you develop values.

Sometimes the main idea of a paragraph is not in the first sentence. In the following paragraph, two important details are underlined. What is the main idea?

Think of how often your hands get dirty. Washing your hands is very important. <u>Always wash your hands before you eat.</u> After you sneeze or cough, be sure to wash your hands. And always wash your hands after using the bathroom. <u>Germs can make you sick.</u>

Skill Practice

Read the following paragraph. Use the Tips for Summarizing to answer the questions.

There are many ways you can protect yourself from the sun. The best way is to always wear sunscreen. You can also wear long pants and shirts with long sleeves. Don't forget a hat with a brim that will shade your face. And, to protect your eyes, you can wear sunglasses.

1 If a friend asked you what this paragraph is about, what information would you include? What would you leave out?

2 What is the main idea of the paragraph?

3 What two details would you include in a summary of the paragraph?

First Aid

For Bleeding—Universal Precautions. . . **296**

For Choking **297**

For Burns **298**

For Nosebleeds. **298**

For Insect Bites and Stings **299**

For Skin Rashes from Plants **299**

For Dental Emergencies **300**

Health and Safety

Backpack Safety **301**

Bike Safety Check. **302**

Safety While Riding **303**

Your Bike Helmet **303**

Safety Near Water **304**

When Home Alone. **306**

For Bleeding–Universal Precautions

You can get some diseases from another person's blood. Avoid touching anyone's blood. To treat a wound, follow the steps below.

If someone is bleeding

1 Wash your hands with soap if possible.

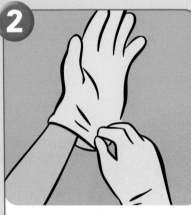

2 Put on protective gloves, if available.

3 Wash small wounds with water. Do not wash serious wounds.

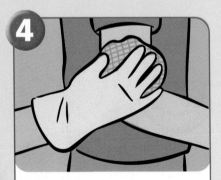

4 Place a clean gauze pad or cloth over the wound. Press firmly for ten minutes. Don't lift the gauze during this time.

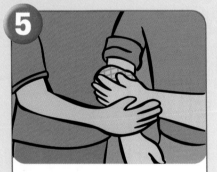

5 If you don't have gloves, have the injured person hold the gauze or cloth in place with his or her hand.

6 If after ten minutes the bleeding has stopped, bandage the wound. If the bleeding has not stopped, continue pressing on the wound and get help.

If you are bleeding, you do not need to avoid your own blood.

For Choking

If someone else is choking

1

Recognize the Universal Choking Sign—grasping the throat with both hands. This sign means a person is choking and needs help.

2

Stand behind the choking person, and put your arms around his or her waist. Place your fist above the person's navel. Grab your fist with your other hand.

3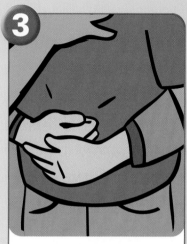

Pull your hands toward yourself, and give five quick, hard, upward thrusts on the person's stomach.

If you are choking when alone

1 Make a fist, and place it above your navel. Grab your fist with your other hand. Pull your hands up with a quick, hard thrust.

2 Or, keep your hands on your belly, lean your body over the back of a chair or over a counter, and shove your fist in and up.

297

For Burns

- Minor burns are called first-degree burns and involve only the top layer of skin. The skin is red and dry, and the burn is painful.

- Second-degree burns cause deeper damage. The burns cause blisters, redness, swelling, and pain.

- Third-degree burns are the most serious because they damage all layers of the skin. The skin is usually white or charred black. The area may feel numb because the nerve endings have been destroyed.

All burns need immediate first aid.

Minor Burns

- Run cool water over the burn or soak it for at least five minutes.

- Cover the burn with a clean dry bandage.

- Do *not* put lotion or ointment on the burn.

More Serious Burns

- Cover the burn with a cool, wet bandage or cloth.

- Do *not* break any blisters.

- Do *not* put lotion or ointment on the burn.

- Get help from an adult right away.

For Nosebleeds

- Sit down, and tilt your head forward. Pinch your nostrils together for at least ten minutes.

- You can also put a cloth-covered cold pack on the bridge of your nose.

- If your nose continues to bleed, get help from an adult.

For Insect Bites and Stings

- Always tell an adult about bites and stings.

- Scrape out the stinger with your fingernail.

- Wash the area with soap and water.

- A covered ice cube or cold pack will usually take away the pain from insect bites. A paste made from baking soda and water also helps.

- If the bite or sting is more serious and is on an arm or leg, keep the leg or arm dangling down. Apply a cold, wet cloth. Get help immediately.

- If you find a tick on your skin, remove it. Protect your fingers with a tissue or cloth to prevent contact with infectious tick fluids. If you must use your bare hands, wash them right away.

- If the tick has already bitten you, ask an adult to remove it. Using tweezers, an adult should grab the tick as close to your skin as possible and pull the tick out in one steady motion. Do not use petroleum jelly because it may cause the tick to struggle releasing its infectious fluids. Wash the bite site.

For Skin Rashes from Plants

Many poisonous plants have three leaves. Remember, "Leaves of three, let them be." If you touch a poisonous plant, wash the area and your hands. If a rash develops, follow these tips.

- Apply calamine lotion or a baking soda and water paste. Try not to scratch. Tell an adult.

- If you get blisters, do not pop them. If they burst, keep the area clean and dry. If your rash does not go away in two weeks, or if the rash is on your face or in your eyes, see your doctor.

For Dental Emergencies

You should know what to do if you have a dental emergency.

Broken Tooth

- Rinse your mouth with warm water. Wrap a cold pack with a cloth. Place it on the injured area. Save any parts of the broken tooth. Call your dentist immediately.

Knocked-Out Permanent Tooth

- Find the tooth and clean it carefully. Handle it by the top (crown), not the root. Put it back into the socket if you can. Hold it in place by biting on clean cloth. If the tooth cannot be put back in, place it in a cup with milk or water. See a dentist immediately. Time is very important in saving the tooth.

Bitten Tongue or Lip

- Apply pressure to the bleeding area with a cloth. Use a cold pack covered with a cloth to stop swelling. If the bleeding doesn't stop within 15 minutes, go to a hospital emergency room.

Food/Objects Caught Between Teeth

- Use dental floss to gently take out the object. Never use anything sharp to take out an object that is stuck between your teeth. If it cannot be removed, call your dentist.

Backpack Safety

Carrying a backpack that is too heavy can injure your back. Carrying one incorrectly also can hurt you.

Safe Weight

A full backpack should weigh no more than 10 to 15 percent of your body weight. Less is better. To find 10 percent, divide your body weight by 10. Here are some examples:

Your Weight (pounds)	Maximum Backpack Weight (pounds)
60	6
65	$6\frac{1}{2}$
70	7

This is the right way to carry a backpack.

Safe Use

- Use a pack with wide shoulder straps and a padded back.

- Lighten your load. Leave unnecessary items at home.

- Pack heavier items inside the pack so that they will be closest to your back.

- Always use both shoulder straps to carry the pack.

- Never wear a backpack while riding a bicycle. The weight makes it harder to stay balanced. Use the bicycle basket or saddlebags instead.

This is the wrong way to carry a backpack.

Bike Safety Check

A safe bike should be the right size for you.

- You should be able to rest your heel on the pedal when you sit on your bike with the pedal in the lowest position.

- When you are standing astride your bike with both feet flat on the ground, your body should be 2 inches above the bar that goes from the handlebar to the seat.

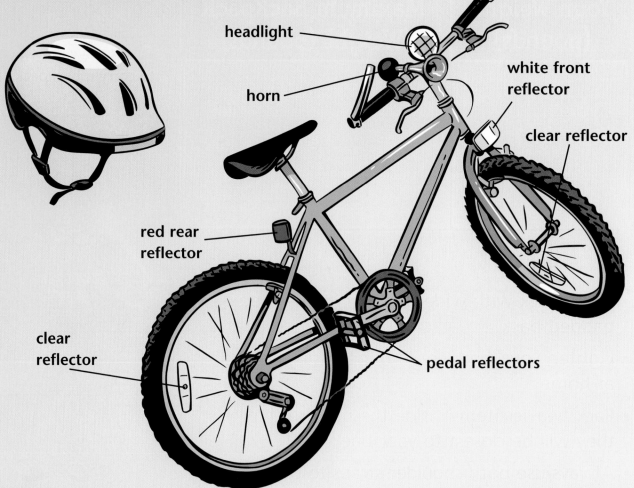

headlight

horn

white front reflector

clear reflector

red rear reflector

clear reflector

pedal reflectors

A bike should have all the safety equipment shown above. Does *your* bike pass the test?

Safety While Riding

Here are some tips for safe bicycle riding.

- Always wear your bike helmet, even for short distances.
- Check your bike every time you ride it. Is it in safe working condition?
- Ride in single file in the same direction as traffic. Never weave in and out of parked cars.
- Before you enter a street, **STOP**. **Look** left, right, and then left again. **Listen** for any traffic. **Think** before you go.
- Walk your bike across an intersection. **Look** left, right, and then left again. Wait for traffic to pass.
- Obey all traffic signs and signals.
- Do not ride your bike at night without an adult. If you do ride at night, be sure to wear light-colored clothing, use reflectors, and front and rear lights.

Your Bike Helmet

- About 500,000 children are involved in bike-related crashes every year. That's why it's important to always wear your bike helmet.
- Wear your helmet properly. It should lie flat on your head. The straps should be snug so it will stay in place if you fall.
- If you do fall and your helmet hits the ground, replace it—even if it doesn't look damaged. The inner foam lining may be crushed. It might not protect you if you fell again.

Safety near Water

Water can be very dangerous. A person can drown in five minutes or less. The best way to be safe near water is to learn how to swim. You should also follow these rules:

- Never swim without the supervision of a lifeguard or a responsible adult.

- If you cannot swim, stay in shallow water. Do not use a blow-up raft to go into deep water.

- Know the rules for the beach or pool and obey them. Do not run or shove others while you are near the water.

- Never dive in head-first the first time. Go feet-first instead to learn how deep the water is.

Pool Rules

1. Public use of pool is permitted only when a lifeguard is on duty.

2. All patrons must shower before entering the pool.

3. No food, drink, gum, glass, or smoking in the pool or on the deck.

4. No animals in pool or on pool deck.

5. Children under the age of 8 years of age must be accompanied by an adult guardian (age 18 or older). Children under 6 years of age must be accompanied by an adult in the water. THIS INCLUDES THE PLAY POOL.

6. Inappropriate behavior such as horseplay, fighting, or use of abusive language is not permitted.

7. Running is not allowed anywhere in pool area.

8. Diving from the side of the pool in the shallow area is not allowed.

9. Flips or back dives from the side of the pool are not allowed.

10. Only one person at a time is allowed on the diving board. Only one bounce is allowed on the diving board.

11. Only Coast Guard-approved flotation devices may be used in the pool.

12. Use of mask, fins, or snorkel is prohibited.

13. Loitering or playing in or around the locker rooms, showers, or restrooms is not allowed.

14. Only regular, clean bathing suits may be worn. Street clothes are not allowed in the pool.

15. Pool capacity and pool hours are posted at the office.

Protect your skin with sunscreen with an SPF of at least 30. Protect your eyes with sunglasses.

Watch the weather. Get out of the water at once if you see lightning or hear thunder.

Wear a Coast Guard–approved life jacket anytime you are in a boat. Wear one when you ride a personal watercraft, too. Know what to do in an emergency.

When Home Alone

Everyone stays home alone sometimes. When you stay home alone, it's important to know how to take care of yourself. Here are some easy rules to follow that will help keep you safe when you are home by yourself.

Do These Things

- Lock all the doors and windows. Be sure you know how to lock and unlock all the locks.

- If someone who is nasty or mean calls, hang up immediately. Tell an adult about the call when he or she gets home. Your parents may not want you to answer the phone at all.

- If you have an emergency, call 911. Be prepared to describe the problem and to give your full name, address, and telephone number. Follow all instructions given to you. Do not hang up the phone until you are told to do so.

- If you see anyone hanging around outside your home, call a neighbor or the police.

- If you see or smell smoke, go outside right away. If you live in an apartment, do not take the elevator. Go to a neighbor's house, and call 911 immediately.

- Entertain yourself. Time will pass more quickly if you are not bored. Work on a hobby, read a book or magazine, do your homework, or clean your room. Before you know it, an adult will be home.

Do Not Do These Things

- Do NOT use the stove, microwave, or oven unless an adult family member has given you permission, and you know how to use these appliances.

- Do NOT open the door for anyone you don't know or for anyone who is not supposed to be in your home.

- Do NOT talk to strangers on the telephone. Do not tell anyone that you are home alone. If the call is for an adult family member, say that he or she can't come to the phone right now and take a message.

- Do NOT have friends over unless you have permission from your parents or other adult family members.

A telephone with caller ID display can help you decide whether to answer the phone.

Glossary

Numbers in parentheses indicate the pages
on which the words are defined in context.

PRONUNCIATION RESPELLING KEY

Sound	As in	Phonetic Respelling	Sound	As in	Phonetic Respelling	Sound	As in	Phonetic Respelling
a	bat	(BAT)	eye	idea	(eye•DEE•uh)	th	thin	(THIN)
ah	lock	(LAHK)	i	bit	(BIT)	u	pull	(PUL)
air	rare	(RAIR)	ing	going	(GOH•ing)	uh	medal	(MED•uhl)
ar	argue	(AR•gyoo)	k	card	(KARD)		talent	(TAL•uhnt)
aw	law	(LAW)		kite	(KYT)		pencil	(PEN•suhl)
ay	face	(FAYS)	ngk	bank	(BANGK)		onion	(UHN•yuhn)
ch	chapel	(CHAP•uhl)	oh	over	(OH•ver)		playful	(play•fuhl)
e	test	(TEST)	oo	pool	(POOL)		dull	(DUHL)
	metric	(MEH•trik)	ow	out	(OWT)	y	yes	(YES)
ee	eat	(EET)	oy	foil	(FOYL)		ripe	(RYP)
	feet	(FEET)	s	cell	(SEL)	z	bags	(BAGZ)
	ski	(SKEE)		sit	(SIT)	zh	treasure	(TREZH•er)
er	paper	(PAY•per)	sh	sheep	(SHEEP)			
	fern	(FERN)	th	that	(THAT)			

A

abstinence (AB•stuh•nuhns)
Not doing a certain thing; avoiding a behavior that harms health *(166)*

addiction (uh•DIK•shuhn)
A constant need for a drug, making people keep using it even when they want to stop *(197)*

advertising (AD•ver•tyz•ing)
A way companies tell consumers about products *(52)*

aerobic exercise (air•OH•bik EK•ser•syz)
Exercise that strengthens the heart and lungs by making them work harder *(88)*

air pollution (AIR puh•LOO•shuhn)
Harmful materials in the air *(266)*

alcohol (AL•kuh•hawl)
A drug found in beer, wine, and liquor *(202)*

alcoholism (AL•kuh•hawl•iz•uhm)
A disease in which a person can't stop using alcohol *(203)*

allergy (AL•er•jee)
The body's reaction to a substance that is harmless to many other people *(159)*

anger (ANG•ger)
A feeling of being very upset *(224)*

apologize (uh•PAH•luh•jyz)
To say you are sorry *(235)*

asthma (AZ•muh)
A disease that causes people to have difficulty breathing *(160)*

bacteria (bak•TIR•ee•uh)
Living things that are so tiny that they cannot be seen without a microscope *(33, 149)*

balanced diet (BAL•uhnst DY•uht)
A diet made up of a healthful amount of foods from each of the food groups *(64)*

body language (BAH•dee LANG•gwij)
Ways people use their bodies to show their feelings *(219)*

bone (BOHN)
A strong, hard body part that helps support the body *(4)*

brain (BRAYN)
The main organ of the body's nervous system; the control center of the body's activities *(6)*

bully (BUL•ee)
Someone who hurts or frightens others *(113)*

C

caffeine (kaf•EEN)
A drug found in coffee, tea, chocolate, and some soft drinks *(172)*

cancer (KAN•ser)
A disease that makes cells grow out of control *(162, 199)*

cavity (KAV•ih•tee)
A hole in a tooth *(36)*

cell (SEL)
The smallest working part of the body *(18)*

chewing tobacco (CHOO•ing tuh•BA•koh)
Moist tobacco used for chewing *(196)*

clinic (KLIN•ik)
A place where people get health care *(262)*

cocaine (koh•KAYN)
An illegal drug made from the leaves of the coca plant *(185)*

communicable disease (kuh•MYOO•nih•kuh•buhl dih•ZEEZ)
A disease that can be spread from one person to another *(148)*

communicate (kuh•MYOO•nuh•kayt)
To share information *(234)*

community (kuh•MYOO•nuh•tee)
A place where people live, work, play, and go to school *(260)*

compassion (kuhm•PA•shuhn)
The ability to understand how others feel *(235)*

consumer (kuhn•SOOM•er)
A person who chooses or buys products *(46)*

cool-down (KOOL•down)
Slow exercise and stretching after exercise to help prevent muscle soreness later *(93)*

D

dental floss (DEN•tuhl FLAWS)
A kind of thread used to remove plaque from between the teeth *(38)*

diabetes (dy•uh•BEET•eez)
A noncommunicable disease that prevents the body from using sugar properly *(161)*

diaphragm (DY•uh•fram)
A thin, flat muscle under the ribs that helps move air in and out of the lungs *(8)*

diet (DY•uht)
The foods a person usually eats and drinks *(62)*

disaster (dih•ZAS•ter)
An event that causes great damage, such as an earthquake or a tornado *(136)*

disease (dih•ZEEZ)
An illness that makes the body unable to work properly *(146)*

divorce (duh•VAWRS)
A legal end to a marriage *(247)*

drug (DRUHG)
A substance, other than food, that changes the way the body works *(172)*

ear canal (IR kuh•NAL)
The part of the outer ear through which sound waves enter *(42)*

eardrum (IR•druhm)
A thin membrane at the inner end of the ear canal; it is moved back and forth by sound waves *(42)*

electricity (ih•lek•TRIS•uh•tee)
A form of energy that can produce light, heat, and motion *(130)*

emergency (ih•MER•juhnt•see)
A situation in which help is needed right away *(126)*

emotions (ih•MOH•shuhnz)
Feelings *(220)*

endurance (en•DUR•uhns)
The ability to exercise for a long time without getting tired *(86)*

environment (en•VY•ruhn•muhnt)
Everything, living and nonliving, around you *(264)*

environmental tobacco smoke (en•vy•ruhn•MEN•tuhl tuh•BA•koh SMOHK)
The smoke that fills an area when someone is smoking *(200)*

esophagus (ih•SAHF•uh•guhs)
The tube made of muscle that squeezes food into the stomach *(10)*

exercise (EK•ser•syz)
Any activity that makes your body work hard *(86)*

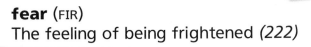

fear (FIR)
The feeling of being frightened *(222)*

feelings (FEE•lingz)
The emotions a person has about people and events *(216)*

flexibility (flek•suh•BIL•uh•tee)
The ability to move or bend easily *(86)*

fluoride (FLAWR•eyed)
A chemical that makes teeth stronger and harder *(39)*

grief (GREEF)
A deep sadness *(225)*

groundwater (GROWND•waw•ter)
Water that sinks into the soil and fills cracks and spaces buried in rocks *(270)*

growth rate (GROHTH RAYT)
The speed at which a person grows *(20)*

hazard (HAZ•uhrd)
A danger that could lead to an injury *(108)*

health department (HELTH dih•PART•muhnt)
A group made up of health workers who work for the government and serve the community *(260)*

health screenings (HELTH SKREEN•ingz)
Tests that check for diseases *(262)*

hospital (HAHS•piht•uhl)
A place where people who are hurt or ill get medical treatment *(261)*

immunity (ih•MYOON•uh•tee)
The body's ability to fight off certain pathogens *(153)*

ingredients (in•GREE•dee•uhnts)
The things that make up a food *(72)*

inhalants (in•HAYL•uhnts)
Substances that give off fumes *(182)*

injury (IN•juh•ree)
Harm done to a person's body *(108)*

label (LAY•buhl)
The wording on a food package that lists the ingredients *(73)*

large intestine (LARJ in•TES•tuhn)
Hollow tube in the lower part of the digestive system in which wastes are stored until they leave the body *(11)*

life cycle (LYF SY•kuhl)
Four stages of growth that people go through *(14)*

limit (LIH•muht)
A point at which a person must stop doing something *(108)*

littering (LIH•ter•ing)
Dropping trash on the ground or in the water *(274)*

liver (LIH•ver)
An organ that makes a liquid that helps the stomach break down food *(11)*

lungs (LUHNGZ)
Large, spongy organs used for breathing, located in the chest *(8)*

marijuana (mair•uh•WAH•nuh)
An illegal drug made from the hemp plant *(184)*

medicines (MED•uh•suhnz)
A liquid, powder, cream, spray, or pill used to treat illness *(154, 172)*

mouth guard (MOWTH GARD)
A plastic shield worn in the mouth to protect the teeth during active sports *(94)*

muscle (MUH•suhl)
A body part that causes movement *(5)*

MyPyramid (MEYE•PIR•uh•mid)
A tool developed by the USDA that helps people choose foods for a healthful diet *(64)*

need (NEED)
Something you must have to live *(218)*

nerves (NERVZ)
Bundles of cells that carry messages to and from the brain *(6)*

nicotine (NIK•uh•teen)
A dangerous drug in tobacco *(197)*

noise pollution (NOYZ puh•LOO•shuhn)
Disturbing or harmful sounds made by human activities *(265)*

noncommunicable disease (nahn•kuh•MYOO•nih•kuh•buhl dih•ZEEZ)
A disease that is not caused by pathogens and cannot be caught from or spread to other people *(158)*

nutrients (NOO•tree•uhnts)
The parts of food that help the body grow and get energy *(61)*

nutrition (noo•TRISH•uhn)
The study of food and how it affects the body *(61)*

O

organ (AWR•guhn)
A group of tissues that work together to do a certain job *(19)*

organ system (AWR•guhn SIS•tuhm)
A group of organs that work together to do a certain job *(19)*

over-the-counter medicine (OH•ver•thuh•kown•ter MED•uh•suhn)
Medicines adults can buy without a doctor's order *(174)*

P

passenger (PA•suhn•jer)
A person who rides in a car or bus with a driver *(109)*

pathogens (PATH•uh•juhnz)
Germs that cause disease *(148)*

peer pressure (PIR PREH•sher)
Peers trying to get you to do something; it can be good or bad *(230)*

peers (PIRZ)
People your own age *(230)*

plaque (PLAK)
A sticky coating that is always forming on teeth *(36)*

poison (POY•zuhn)
A substance that causes illness, injury, or death when it gets on the skin or into the body *(128)*

pollution (puh•LOO•shuhn)
Something that makes the environment unhealthful *(264)*

pollution control technician (puh•LOO•shuhn kuhn•TROHL tek•NIH•shuhn)
A person who tests water, air, or soil for harmful substances *(266)*

pores (PAWRZ)
Tiny holes in the skin *(32)*

prescription medicine (prih•SKRIP•shuhn MED•uh•suhn)
Medicine that a doctor orders for you *(175)*

private (PRY•vuht)
Belonging to a certain person *(26)*

recycle (ree•SY•kuhl)
To collect used things so they can be made into new things *(277)*

reduce (rih•DOOS)
To make less of something *(275)*

reuse (ree•YOOZ)
To use something again *(276)*

refuse (rih•FYOOZ)
To say *no* *(189)*

relationship (rih•LAY•shuhn•ship)
The way one person gets along with another person *(228)*

responsibilities (rih•spahn•suh•BIL•uh•teez)
Things that someone expects you to do *(252)*

role (ROHL)
The part you play in your family *(253)*

safety gear (SAYF•tee GIR)
Clothing or equipment that helps protect you *(92)*

safety rules (SAYF•tee ROOLZ)
Rules that protect people from injury *(108)*

self-control (self•kuhn•TROHL)
Power over your emotions *(220)*

sibling (SIB•ling)
A brother or sister *(246)*

side effect (SYD ih•FEKT)
Unwanted changes in the body, caused by a medicine *(175)*

skeletal system (SKEL•uh•tuhl SIS•tuhm)
The bones; the hard parts of the body that support and protect the softer parts *(4)*

small intestine (SMAWL in•TES•tuhn)
The hollow tube between the stomach and the large intestine; through this tube the body absorbs the nutrients in foods *(11)*

smokeless tobacco (SMOHK•lis tuh•BA•koh)
Powdered or shredded tobacco that people put between their cheeks and gums *(196)*

snacks (SNAKS)
Foods eaten between meals *(69)*

spinal cord (SPY•nuhl KAWRD)
The bundle of nerves that carries messages between the brain and the rest of the nerves in the body *(6)*

spoiled (SPOYLD)
Unsafe to eat *(79)*

stomach (STUH•muhk)
The organ, between the esophagus and the small intestine, that mixes food
with juices and squeezes it into a thick liquid *(11)*

stranger (STRAYN•jer)
A person you do not know *(112)*

strength (STRENGTH)
The power of your muscles *(86)*

stress (STRES)
A feeling of worry and nervousness *(223)*

sunscreen (SUHN•skreen)
A product that keeps the sun's rays from burning your skin *(35)*

symptom (SIMP•tuhm)
A sign that something is wrong with the body *(146)*

tar (TAR)
A dark, sticky substance that coats the lungs and air passages of people who breathe tobacco smoke *(199)*

tendon (TEN•duhn)
A band of tough material that attaches a muscle to a bone *(5)*

tissue (TISH•OO)
A group of cells of the same kind that work together *(19)*

trachea (TRAY•kee•uh)
The tube that carries air from the nose and mouth into the lungs; also called the windpipe *(8)*

trusted adult (TRUHST•uhd uh•DUHLT)
A grown-up you know well or an adult in a responsible position *(115)*

vaccine (vak•SEEN)
A substance that can keep a person from getting a certain disease *(153)*

values (VAL•yooz)
Strong beliefs and actions that are important to a family *(244)*

virus (VY•ruhs)
A tiny pathogen that causes disease *(149)*

want (WAWNT)
Something you would like to have but don't need *(218)*

warm-up (WAWRM•uhp)
Stretching and slow exercises to get muscles ready for exercise to prevent pulled muscles *(92)*

water pollution (WAW•ter puh•LOO•shuhn)
Harmful materials in lakes, oceans, or rivers *(269)*

Index

Boldfaced numbers refer to illustrations.

Actions, to show feelings, 219

Addiction. *See also* Drugs; Illegal drugs
to alcohol, 203
defined, 197
to tobacco, 197

Adults
safety rules from, **108**
trusted, 115, **115**

Advertising, 52, 53
analyzing, 52, 74
defined, 52
by famous people, 46
types of, 52–53

Aerobic exercise, 87, 88

Air pollution, 266

Alcohol
car crashes related to, **203**
defined, 202
effects on body systems, **204,** 204–205
harm from, 203
kinds of, 202
laws about using, 210
learning about, 202–205
refusing, 206–207, **206–207, 208,** 208–209, **209**

Alcoholism, 203

Allergy, 159
defined, 159
shots for, 159

Anger
defined, 224
managing, 224
myth and fact about, 220
stress and, **224**

Animals
food from, 60
littering and, **275**

Antibiotics, 178

Apologizing, 234, 235

Aspirin, safety of, 178

Asthma, 160
and refusing tobacco, 166

Audiologist, 55

Baby
family changes caused by, **246,** 247
giving birth in a hospital, **261**

Backup noises, from vehicles, **120**

Bacteria, 33, 150
communicable diseases from, 149
defined, 33, 149
in plaque, 36
water pollution and, 270

Balanced diet, 64, **64–65,** 66

Bathing, 33

Biking, 93
safety equipment for, 118
safety in, 261

Blizzard, 137, **137**

Body language
communicating through, **235**
defined, 219
feelings and, 219

Body systems
digestive system, **10,** 10–11
effects of alcohol on, 203, **204,** 204–205
effects of cocaine on, 185

effects of illegal drugs on, 184, 185
effects of inhalants on, 183, **183**
effects of noise pollution on, 265
effects of tobacco on, **198,** 198–199, **199**
muscular system, 5, **5**
nervous system, 6, **6,** 12
organ systems, 19
respiratory system, 8–9, **9**
rest and, 100, 102
skeletal system, 4, **4**
working together, 7, 12–13

Body temperature, 146, **146**

Bones. *See also* Skeletal system
defined, 4

Brain
biking injury to, 261
cell growth in, 20
defined, 6
effects of alcohol on, 203, 204, **204,** 205
effects of cocaine on, 185
effects of marijuana on, 184
rest and, 100

Bread, pasta, rice, and cereal group, 66, **66,** 67

Breath, tobacco and, **199**

Breathing, 8–9
asthma and, 160, **160**

Bully, 113
communicating about, **222**
defined, 113

Bus, passenger safety in, 109, **109**

Buying decisions, hobbies to help cope with stress, 223

C

Caffeine, 173, 176
  avoiding, 177
  in common products,
    176
  defined, 172
  myth and fact about,
    177

Calcium, 4

Cancer, 162
  defined, 199
  skin, 34
  tobacco and, 199, **199**

Car
  alcohol-related crashes,
    203
  hybrid, 266, **266**
  passenger safety in, 109,
    109

Carbohydrates, 62

Carbon dioxide, 8

Cavities, 37

Celebrations, rituals in,
    244

Cells, 19, **19**
  in brain, 20
  cancer, 162
  defined, 18
  in skin surface, 19, **19**
  viruses in, 149

Checkup, 25, **153**
  at clinic, 262

Chemicals, groundwater
    pollution from, 270

Chewing tobacco, 196

Choking, 133, **133**

Cigarettes, myth and fact
    about, 196

Citizenship, obeying rules
    and laws for safety, 129

Cleaning products
  caution labels on, 183
  fumes from, 182
  poison safety and, 128
  safety of, 173

Cleanliness, 25
  of ears, 43
  good grooming habits
    and, 41
  of skin, **32**, 33
  washing fruits and
    vegetables, **78**

Clinic, 262

Clothing, for sun
    protection, **34**

Cocaine, 185

Colds
  as communicable
    diseases, 150
  myth and fact about, 8
  treating, 154

**Communicable
  diseases,** 150
  from bacteria, 149
  defined, 148
  fever and, 155
  from viruses, 149

Communicating,
  about alcohol, 202
  apologizing as, **234**
  body language for, **235**
  about bully, **222**
  about community helper,
    263
  about dangerous
    situations, 181
  defined, 134, 234
  in emergency, 134–135,
    134–135, 139
  in families, 96, 243, **243**
  about feelings, 22–23,
    22–23, 218
  about grief, **225**
  about inhalants, 182
  about injuries, 96, 97
  as life skill, 113
  listening skills and, 236,
    236
  about school safety, 110,
    111
  about sore throat, 262
  about stress, **157**, 223
  about symptoms, 154
  types of communication,
    234, 234–235, **235**
  about weapons, 114

Community
  defined, 260
  health and safety helpers
    in, 263, **263**
  health services in,
    260–263
  setting goals to improve,
    272–273, **272–273**

Comparison shopping
  for prices, 74
  for soups, **73**

Compassion, 235

Compromise,
  to resolve conflicts, **251**

Conflict resolution,
  with friends, 231
  by listening to others,
    250–251, **250–251**
  using negotiation,
    116–117, **116–117**

Consumer,
  defined, 46

Consumer awareness
  access valid health
    information, 176, 265
  alcohol and, 209
  analyzing advertising
    messages, 74
  analyzing media
    messages, 52, 74
  buying decisions, 223
  about product choices,
    54, 75

Consumer information,
  finding, 54

Cool-down, 93, 94

Coping
  with emotions, 222–225
  with family changes, 248

Crack, 185

Cranberries, 60, **61**

Crown, of tooth, **37**

D

Deaf people
  translator for, **237**
  TTY for, 234

Decay, 37

Decision making,
about buying, 46
about injuries, 132
about safety, 98–99, **98–99**
about snacks, 76–77, **76–77**

Dental floss, 38, **38**

Dentin, of tooth, **37**

Dentists, 25

Diabetes, 161

Diaphragm, 8, **9**

Diet
for diabetes, 161
food groups and, 66–67
healthful, 164, **164**
serving sizes and, 66–67

Digestive system, 10–11
caring for, 11
parts of, 10, **10**
unhealthful habits for, **11**

Disability, 147
caring for people who
are ill, 163
defined, 147
from illness, 147

Disaster
defined, 136
emergency list for, 138
safety in, **136**, 136–137,
137

Disease. See also Illness
alcoholism as, 203
caring for people with,
163
causes of, 148–151
communicable, 148, 150
defined, 146
learning about, 146–147
noncommunicable,
158–162
preventing, 152–153
stress management for
controlling, 156–157,
156–157
tobacco and, **199**
treating, **154**, 154–155

Divorce, 246

Doctors
checkups and, 25
injuries and, 97
pediatricians as, **27**
prescription medicines
and, 175, **175**
surgeons as, 261

Dreaming, 101

Drinking. See Alcohol

Driving, drinking and, 203

Drugs
defined, 172
harmful and illegal,
182–185
illegal, 173, **184,**
184–185, **185**
kinds of drugs, 172–173
learning about, 172–177
as medicines, 172
nicotine, 197
saying no to drugs, **188,**
188–190, **189, 190**

Ear canal, 42

Eardrum, 42

Ears
caring for, 42–43
damage to, **42, 43**

Earthquakes, 136, 139,
139
myth and fact about,
136

Eating, 24
digestive system and,
10–11
healthful, 164, **164**

Electrical storm, 137,
137, 139, **139**

Electricity
defined, 130
in kitchen, 131
safety around, 130

Emergency
choking, 133, **133**
communicating during,
134–135, **134–135,** 139
defined, 126
family meeting place in,
127
fire as, 126
fire escape map and, **126**
first-aid kit for, 132, **132**
insect stings, 133
planning for, 138, **138**

Emergency rooms, 261

Emotions. See also
Feelings
anger, 224
coping with, 222–225
fear, 222
grief, 225
stress, 223

Enamel, of tooth, **37**

Endurance, 86

Energy, from food, 61

Environment
air pollution and, 266
defined, 264
healthful, 264–266
maintaining health of,
278
noise pollution and, **264,**
265
pollution of, 264
protecting, **274,** 274–278
recycling and, 277, **277**
reducing littering and,
275, **275**
reusing materials and,
276, **276**
setting goals to improve,
272–273, **272–273**
water pollution and,
268–271

**Environmental tobacco
smoke (ETS),** 200, 210

Esophagus, 10, **10**

ETS. See Environmental
tobacco smoke (ETS)

Exercise, 4, 24, **87,** 165
aerobic, **87,** 88
defined, 86

drinking water during, 93
effects of, 90
for fitness, 88
with friends, **90**
for fun, 89
injuries from, 96–97
jumping rope as, **89**
myth and fact about, 89
safety during, 92–95
stress and, 165
stretching, 92, **92**, **93**

Eyes, protecting, 44, **44**

Family
changes in, 246–249
communicating in, 243, **243**, 263
emergency escape route for, 126, **126**
emergency meeting place, 127, **127**
fire escape map and, **126**
fun in, 254, **254**
helping each other in, 244
helping you say *no* to drugs, 190, **190**
learning about, 242–244
making a happy home and, **242**
new baby in, **246**, 247
new people in, **248**
number of children in, **247**
relationship with, **228**, 228–229, **229**
resolving conflicts with, 250–251, **250–251**
responsibilities in, 252
role in, 253, **253**
safety rules from, **108**
telling about injury, 96
values in, 244
ways family members help each other, 252–254

Family Day, 242
Fats, 62
Fats, oils, sweets group, 62, 66, **66**
Fear, coping with, 222
Feelings, 216. *See also* Emotions
anger, 220
communicating about, 22–23, **22–23**, 218
dealing with uncomfortable feelings, 221
defined, 216
feeling good about yourself, 216–217
positive influence on, **220**
teasing and, 243
understanding, 216–221
ways to control feelings, 220–221
ways to show feelings, 219, **219**
Fever, 155
medicines for, 178
Fire
clothing fire, 127, **127**
escaping from, 127, **127**
safety in, 126
Firefighter, 279
First aid, 132, 132–133, **133**
Fitness, exercise for, 88
Flavored cigarettes, 196
Flexibility, 86, **87**
Flu, 150
medicines for, 178
treating, 154
Fluoride, 39
Food
from animals, 60
with caffeine, 172, 177
calcium in, 4

comparing prices of, 74
comparing products, 73
digestive system and, 10–11
freshness of, 61
healthful, **68**, 68–70, **69**
importance of, 61
labels on, 72, **72**, 73, **73**, 75
nutrients in, 62–63, **62–63**
packaged, 72
from plants, 60
refrigerating, 80, **80**
safe handling of, **78–79**, 78–80
shopping for, 72–75
storing, 79, **79**
where food comes from, 60
wrapping or storing in covered containers, **79**
Food groups, serving sizes and, **66**, 66–67
Food guide pyramid, 64, **64–65**, 69
See also **MyPyramid**
Food guides, 64
Food inspector, 81
Friends
being a good friend, 233
choosing, 232
exercising with, **90**
myth and fact about, 230
peer pressure and, 230
qualities of, 232
relationships with, **230**, 230–231, **231**
resolving conflicts with, 231
Fruit
washing, **78**
Fruit food group, 67
Fumes, as poisons, 173, 182, 183
Fun, in families, 254, **254**

Garbage, packaging as, 275

Germs
  colds and, 8
  from dirt, 25
  on foods, 78
  food storage and, 79

Goal setting, 24
  for choosing health-care products, 50–51, **50–51**
  to improve environment, 272–273, **272–273**

Grief, coping with, 225, **225**

Grooming, 41, **41**

Groundwater, pollution of, 270, **270**

Growth, 14–16, 18–21
  process of, 18

Growth rate, **18**, 20, **20**

Gum, 37

Gymnastics, 88

Habits, good health, 24–25, **24–25**

Hand washing, **32**, 33
  to prevent disease, 152, **152**

Harmful drugs, 182–183

Hazard, defined, 108

Head lice, 151
  preventing, **151**

Health, good habits for, 24–25, **24–25**

Health care
  from clinics, 262, **262**
  from community helpers, 263, **263**
  finding, 260–263
  from health departments, 260, **260**
  from hospitals, 261, **261**

Health-care products, **46**, 46–49
  added ingredients in, 49
  comparing, 48, **48**
  making choices about, 50–51, **50–51**, 54
  purchasing decisions for, 46, **46**
  reading labels on, 47, **47**
  value and sizes of, 48–49

Health department, 260, **260**

Healthful food
  lunch, 71
  for meals, 68, **68**
  snacks, 69, **69**, 70

Healthful lifestyle, **164**, 164–166
  avoiding tobacco, 166
  eating a healthful diet, 164, **164**
  exercising often, 165, **165**
  stress management for, 226–227, **226–227**

Health information, 96, 118
  accessing valid information, 176, 265

Health screenings, at clinics, 262

Heart
  effects of alcohol on, **204**
  effects of marijuana on, 184
  effects of tobacco on, **198**, **199**
  rest and, 102

Helmet, 94, **94**
  for biking, 261
  buying of, 119, **119**

Helping, in families, 252–254

Herbal medicines, myth and fact about, 173

Home
  happy family in, **242**

safety in, **130**, 130–133, **131**, **132**, **133**
  someone moving into, **247**

Honesty, 217

Hospital, 261, **261**

Human body, changes in, 16, **16**

Human life cycle, 14–15
  adult to senior, 15, **15**
  birth to two, 14, **14**
  defined, 14
  ten to adult, 15, **15**
  two to ten, 15, **15**

Hurricane, **136**, 137, 139, **139**

Hybrid cars, 266, **266**

Illegal drugs, 173, **184**, 184–185, **185**
  cocaine as, 185, **185**
  marijuana as, 184, **184**, **185**
  saying *no* to drugs, **188**, 188–190, **189**, **190**

Illness. *See also* Disease
  caring for people with, 163
  communicating about, 262
  disability from, 147
  medicines for, **178**
  from nicotine, 197

"I" messages, for resolving conflicts, **250**

Immunity
  defined, 153
  from vaccine, **153**

Infections, marijuana use and, 184

Information. *See* Health information

Ingredients
  on food labels, **72**, 73, 75
  healthful, 75

Inhalants, 182
defined, 182
effects of, 183
refusing, 186–187, **186–187**

Inhalers, for asthma, 160

Injury
defined, 108
in exercise, 96–97
first aid for, **132,** 132–133, **133**
seeing doctor about, 97
sports injuries in children, **119**
from sports on wheels, 118
what to do for, 96

Insect stings, 133

Intestine
effects of alcohol on, **204**
large, 10, **10,** 11
myth and fact about, 12
small, 10, **10,** 11

Journaling, to deal with uncomfortable feelings, 221

Juice, 61
packaging of, **74**

Jumping rope, 89

Kitchen, safety in, 131, **131**

Labels
on alcohol and tobacco products, 210
caution warnings on, 183
defined, 73
food labels and, 72, 73, 75

on inhalants, 182
on OTC medicines, 174
reading, 47, **47**

Lab technician, 167

Large intestine, 10, **10**
compared with small intestine, 12
defined, 11
myth and fact about, 12

Laws. *See also* Rules
obeying for safety, 129
about using alcohol and tobacco, 210

Learning, brain pathways for, 20–21

Lice. *See* Head lice

Life cycle. *See* Human life cycle

Lifeguards, 95

Life skills
communicating, 113, 182, 202, 218, 262
making decisions, 40, 132
managing stress, xii, 87, 90, 156–157, 248
refusing, 166
setting goals, 24, 73

Listening
in family, 243
resolving conflicts with, 250–251, **250–251**

Listening skills,
communicating and, 236, **236**

Listening to music, as rest, 102

Littering, 274
defined, 274
myth and fact about, 274
packaging and, 275
reducing, 275, **275**
reuse of materials and, 276, **276**

Liver, 10, **10**
defined, 11
effects of alcohol on, **204,** 205

Lunch, eating healthful meal, 71

Lungs, 9
asthma and, **160**
defined, 8
effects of cocaine on, 185
effects of marijuana on, 184
effects of tobacco on, **198,** 199, **199**

Magnetic resonance imaging (MRI), 21, **21**

Making choices, about food products, 75

Marijuana, 184

Meals, healthful, 68

Meat, poultry, fish, dry beans, eggs, and nuts group, 66, **66,** 67
safe handling of, 78

Media
advertising in, 52
analyzing messages in, 74

Medicine, 154, **155, 172**
defined, 154, 172
forms of, 180
herbal, 173
over-the-counter, **173,** 174, **174,** 175
prescription, **174,** 175
safe uses of, 178–180, **179**
side effects of, 175
uses of, **178**

Mental growth, 20

Meteorologist, 141

Microwave, safety around, **131**

Midwives, 261

Milk, yogurt, and cheese food group, 67

Minerals, 61, 63

Mouth, 9, 10, **10**
effects of tobacco on, **198**, **199**

Mouth guard, 94, **94**

Moving, family and, 247, **247**, 248

MRI. *See* Magnetic resonance imaging (MRI)

Muscle, 5
exercise and, 86
rest and, 100

Muscular system, 5, **5**
working with other systems, 7

MyPyramid, 64, **64–65**, 69

Native Americans, tea from willow bark and, 172

Needs, 218
wants and, **218**

Negotiating, to resolve conflicts, 116–117, **116–117**, **251**

Neonatal nurse, 255

Nerve cells, 20

Nerves, 6

Nervous system, 6, 12
working with other systems, 7

Nicotine, 198
defined, 197
as insect killer, **197**, **911**, 127, **127**

NOAA Weather Radio, 138

Noise
harm from, **42**, 43
identifying, 42

Noise pollution, 264, 265

Noncommunicable disease, 158–162
allergy, 159
asthma, 160

cancer, 162
defined, 158
diabetes, 161

Nose, 9
protecting, 45

Nosebleed, 45

Nurses
neonatal, **255**
public health, **260**

Nutrients, 68
defined, 61
in foods, 62, **62**

Nutrition, 61. *See also* Eating; Food

Organ, 19

Organ system, 19

Over-the-counter medicines (OTC), 173, 174, **174**, 175

Packaged foods, 72

Packaging, 74
advertising and, 53
as garbage, 275

Passenger, 109, **109**

Pathogens
communicable diseases from, 149
defined, 148
immunity to, 153
spreading, **148**, **149**
washing hands and, 152, **152**

Pediatrician, 27

Peer pressure, 230

Personality, alcohol and, 204–205

Pharmacist, 175, **175**, 191

Pharmacy, doctor's prescriptions and, 175, **175**

Physical activity. *See* Exercise; Sports

Physical education teacher, 103

Physical therapists, 97

Physician. *See* Doctors

Planning for emergencies, 138, **138**

Plants, as food, 60

Plaque, 36

Plastics, recycling of, 277, **277**

Play
exercise and, **87**, 89
safety for, 94–95

Poison
fumes as, 173
nicotine as, 197, **197**
safety around, 128, **128**

Pollution. *See also* Environment
air, 266
defined, 264
groundwater, 270, **270**
noise, **264**, 265
water, 268–271

Pollution control technician, 266

Pores, 32

Prescription medicine, 174, 175

Prices, comparison shopping for, 74

Privacy, 26

Product labels, 47, **47**
for foods, 72, 73

Proteins, 61, 62

Public health nurses, 260

Public health workers, 260

Pulp, of tooth, 37, **37**

Reading, as rest, 102, **102**

Recycling, 277, **277**
of plastics, 277
Refrigeration, of food, **79,** 80
Refusing,
alcohol, 206–207, **206–207, 208,** 208–209, **209**
bad touch, 26
defined, 189
inhalants, 186–187, **186–187**
saying *no* to drugs, **188,** 188–190, **189, 190**
tobacco, 166, 206–207, **206–207, 208,** 208–209, **209**
Relationship
defined, 228
with family, **228,** 228–229, 229
with friends, **230,** 230–231, **231**
Remarriage, 247
REM sleep, 101
Resources, caring for, 278
Respect, 217
for adults, 17, **17**
Respiratory system, 8–9, 9
Respiratory therapist, 211
Responsibilities, 252
Responsible behavior, 217
Rest
during day, 102, **102**
to get better from illness, **150**
sleep and, 100–101
Reusing, 276
Rituals, 244
Road safety, 109, **109**
Role
defined, 253
in family, 253, **253**
Root, of tooth, 37

Rules. *See also* Laws
in family, 244
obeying for safety, 129
safety, 108, 112, 130
of sports and physical activities, 91
about tobacco, 200
for using medicines, 179, **179,** 180
Running, warm up and cool down for, **93**

Safety
from alcohol and tobacco, **208,** 208–209 **209**
of aspirin, 178
in biking, 261
of cleaning products, 173
community helpers for, 263
in disasters, **136, 137,** 136–141
around electricity, 130
during exercise, 92–95
in fires, 127, **127**
in food handling, **78–79,** 78–80
in home, **130,** 130–133, **131, 132, 133**
in kitchen, 131, **131**
making decisions about, 98–99, **98–99**
around others, **112,** 112–113
in play, 94
around poisons, 128
on road, 109, **109**
at school, 110, 111
in using medicines, 178–180
vehicle, 120, **120**
in wheeled sports, 118, 119
Safety belt, 109
Safety gear, 25
for biking, 93, 118
defined, 92
for ears, 43, **43**
for eyes, 44, **44**

helmets as, 119, **119**
mouth guard as, 94, **94**
for scooters, 118
for skateboarding, 118
for skating, 118
for teeth, 40
Safety rules, 108
Saying no to alcohol and tobacco, 209, 209
Saying no to drugs, 188, 188–190, **189, 190**
people who can help you, 190, **190**
reasons to say *no,* 188
ways to say *no,* 189, **189**
School
safety at, 110, 111
taking pride in, 267, **267**
Scooters, safety gear for, 118
Security guard, 121
Self-control, 220–221
Sewage, 268
Sewage treatment plant, 268, **268–269**
Shampoo, 46
comparing prices of, 48, **48,** 49
Shopping, for food, 72–75
Sibling, 247
Side effects
defined, 175
of inhalants, **182–183**
Skateboarding, safety gear for, 118
Skating, safety gear for, 118
Skeletal system, 4, 7, 12
defined, 4
working with other systems, 7, 12
Skin
caring for, 32–35
cleanliness of, 32–33
protecting from sun, **34,** 34–35
surface of, 19, **19**

Skin cancer, 34

Sleep, 9, 24, **100**
exercise and, 90
hours needed, 101, **101**
as rest, 100–101
stages of, 101

Small intestine, 10, **10**
compared with large intestine, 11, 12
defined, 11
effects of alcohol on, **204**
myth and fact about, 12

Smokeless tobacco, 196

Smoking. *See* Tobacco

Snacks, 70
appetite and, 69
deciding about, 76–77, **76–77**
healthful, 69, **69**

Sound, harm from, **42**, 43

Soups, comparing, 73

Spinal cord, 6

Sports, 89. *See also* Exercise
safety gear for, 94, **94**

Sprains, 96

Stepparents, 247

Stomach, 10, **10**
defined, 11
effects of alcohol on, **204**

Storage of food, 79

Store brands, 74

Storms, electrical, 137, **137**

Stranger
defined, 112
safety around, **112**, 112–113

Strength, 86, **87**

Stress
anger and, **224**
communicating about, 223
defined, 223

Stress management, 87, 248

for disease control, 156–157, **156–157**
with exercise, 90
for health, 226–227, **226–227**

Stretching, **93**
exercises, **92**

Sugar, and diabetes, 161

Sunburn, 34, **35**

Sunglasses, 35, 44

Sunscreen, 34, 35

Surgeons, 261

Sweating, 93

Swimming, 95

Symptoms
allergy shots for, 159
of cold, 150
communicating about, 154
defined, 146
fever, 155
of flu, 150
medicines for, 178, **178**

Talking, to deal with uncomfortable feelings, 221

Tar
from cigarettes, **198**, 199
defined, 199

Teacher
helping you say *no* to drugs, 190, **190**
safety rules from, **108**

Teasing, 243

Technology
alcohol and, 205
disaster information and, 138
electric toothbrushes and, 37
food freshness and, 61
hybrid cars, 266, **266**
lifeguards and, 95
TTY (Text Telephone Yoke) and, 234

vehicle backup sounds, **120**

Teeth, 37
brushing, 39, **39**
caring for, 25, 36–40
decay of, 37
healthy, **36**
losing, 40
parts of, **37**
protecting, 40
tobacco and, **199**

Temperature, 140. *See also* Body temperature

Tendon, 5

Terrorism, 137

Thermometer, 146

Throat, effects of tobacco on, **198**

Tissue, 19

Tobacco, 196
addiction to, 197
avoiding, 166
chewing tobacco, 196
effects on body, **198**, **199**, 198–199
harm to nonusers, 200
laws about using, 210
learning about, 196–200
refusing, 206–207, **206–207**, **208**, 208–209, **209**
respiratory system and, 8
smoke from, 199
smokeless tobacco, 196
smoking of, 196
tar in, **198**, 199

Toothbrush, 39
electric, 37

Tornado, 136, 139, **139**

Touching, good and bad, 26, **26**

Toxic substances, pollution and, 271

Trachea, 8, **9**

Translator for the deaf, 237

Treatment, of disease, **154**, 154–155

Trusted adults
communicating about alcohol with, 202
communicating with, 263
defined, 115, **115**
helping you say *no* to drugs, 190, **190**
reporting dangerous situations to, 181

TTY (Text Telephone Yoke), 234

United States Department of Agriculture (USDA)
Food Guide Pyramid, 64

Unit price, 74, 75

Vaccination, at clinic, 262

Vaccine, 153, **153**

Value of health-care products
myth and fact about, 49

Values (personal), 244, **244**

Vegetable food group, 67

Vegetables
washing, **78**

Vehicle safety, 120, **120**

Violence, avoiding, 114

Virus
cold from, 150
defined, 149

Visualization, for stress management, **157**

Vitamins, 61, 62

Walking, safety for, **109**

Wants, 218
needs and, **218**

Warm-up, 92, 94
defined, 92

Warning signs, obeying, 129

Washing. *See* Cleanliness

Waste, 10, 11
recycling, 277, **277**
reducing, 275, **275**
reusing materials, 276, **276**

Water
as nutrient, 61, 63
sweating and, 93
swimming safety and, 95

Water pollution
controlling, 268–271
of groundwater, 270, **270**
myth and fact about, 270
stopping, 271, **271**

Weapons, avoiding, 114, **114**

Weather, being prepared for, 140

Weather Radio, 138

Weight, healthful diet and, 164

Wheeled sports
injuries from, **119**
safety with, 118, 119

Words, to show feelings, 219

Workout, defined, 93

X rays, 21

CREDITS

Cover Design: Bill Smith Studio

Photographs:

KEY: (t) top, (b) bottom, (l) left, (r) right, (c) center, (bg) background, (fg) foreground

Cover Photographer: Brian Fraunfelter

13 Getty Images; 14 David Young-Wolff/PhotoEdit; 15 (t) Getty Images; 15 (c) Cleve Bryant/PhotoEdit; 15 (b) George Shelley/Corbis; 19 (tl) Carolina Biological Supply Company/Phototake; 19 (bl) James Hayden, RBP/Phototake; 19 (br) Science Photo Library/Photo Researchers; 21 Jack Plekan/Fundamental Photographs; 56 (tl) David Young-Wolff/PhotoEdit; 60 (l) George D. Lepp/Corbis; 60 (r) Richard Hamilton Smith/Corbis; 61 (t) GoodShot/Superstock; 61 (c) Ulrike Welsch/Photo Researchers; 89 Richard Hutchings/PhotoEdit; 90 Getty Images; 103 David Young-Wolff/PhotoEdit/PictureQuest; 108 (l) Rob Lewine/Corbis; 108 (c) Ken Cavanagh/Photo Researchers; 108 (r) David Yound-Wolff/PhotoEdit; 122 (bl) Parrot Pascal/Corbis Sygma; 135 (l) Michael Newman/PhotoEdit; 136 (l) Roger Ressmeyer/Corbis; 136 (r) Eric Meola/Getty Images; 136 (bg) Charles O'Rear/Corbis; 137 (l) Marc Epstein/Visuals Unlimited; 137 (r) David Pollack/Corbis; 137 (c) David R. Frazier; 138 (tl) Alan Schein Photography; 138 (cl) Graeme Teague Photography; 138 (bl) Rov vanNostrand; 141 Dwayne Newton/PhotoEdit; 142 (tr) Tom Stewart/Corbis; 142 (br) Laurence Monneret/Getty Images; 148 (l) Science VU/CDC/Visuals Unlimited; 148 (r) Eye of Science/Photo Researchers; 149 (t) Dr. Gopal Murti/Phototake; 149 (b) David M. Phillips/Visuals Unlimited; 160 Bob Daemmrich Photography; 162 Michael Newman/PhotoEdit; 165 (l) SW Productions/Getty Images; 165 (c) Mary Kate Denny/PhotoEdit; 165 (r) Suzanne Haldane/Stock, Boston; 166 James A. Sugar/Corbis; 167 Inga Spence/Visuals Unlimited; 168 (bl) James Darell/Getty Images; 168 (tr) Comstock; 168 (br) Catherine Ledner/Getty Images; 184 (l) Chris Knapton/Alamy Images; 184 (c) Getty Images; 184 (r) Dale C. Spartas/Corbis; 185 Ivan Polunin/Bruce Coleman, Inc.; 185 (inset) David Hoffman/Alamy Images; 188 (r) Paul Barton/Corbis; 191 (l) Bettmann/Corbis; 191 (r) Jeff Kaufman/Getty Images; 192 (tr) Lawrence Manning/Corbis; 192 (br) Sergio Piumatti; 197 (l) Getty Images; 199 (l) Royalty-free/Corbis; 199 (r) Getty Images; 202 (r) Brian Hagiwara/Getty Images; 202 (c) Getty Images; 202 (l) David Prince/Getty Images; 203 Tom Carter/PhotoEdit; 210 David Falconer/Bruce Coleman, Inc.; 211 David Young-Wolff/PhotoEdit; 228 (l) Steve Smith/Superstock; 228 (r) Rob Lewine/Corbis; 230 Dennis O'Clair/Getty Images; 235 Lynne Siler/Focus Group/PictureQuest; 238 LWA-Dann Tardif/Corbis; 255 Pete Saloutos/Corbis; 257 (tl) Royalty-Free/Corbis; 257 (tr) Lawrence Migdale; 257 (br) Myrleen Ferguson Cate/PhotoEdit; 260 (l) ThinkStock/Index Stock Imagery; 260 (r) Amy Etra/PhotoEdit; 261 Getty Images; 268 David R. Frazier; 270 Jim Steinberg/Photo Researchers; 271 Michael Habicht/Animals Animals/Earth Scenes; 275 (l) Doug Perrine/Peter Arnold, Inc.; 275 (r) Buddy Mays/Corbis; 278 Lynda Richardson/Corbis; 279 Spencer Grant/PhotoEdit; 280 (tl) Weronica Ankarorn/Harcourt; 280 (bl) Royalty-Free/Corbis;

All other photos © Harcourt School Publishers. Harcourt photos provided by the Harcourt Index, Harcourt IPR, and Harcourt photographers; Weronica Ankarorn, Victoria Bowen, Eric Camden, Annette Coolidge, Doug Dukane, Ken Kinzie, Brian Minnich, and Steve Williams.

Illustrations:

David Brooks, ix, 282, 284, 286, 288, 290, 292; Karen Stormer Brooks, v, 12, 33, 42-43, 48, 74, 95, 109, 208-209, 217, 219, 228-229, 252; Jean Calder, 4, 5, 6, 9, 10; Mark Collins, vii, viii, 46, 101, 103, 167, 172, 173, 182-183, 211, 213, 230, 237, 255, 261; Mike Dammer, vi, 27, 55, 126, 136, 268, 269, 270; Bob Eckstein, 127, 139; John Karapelou, 19, 37, 57, 160, 198, 204, 212; Chris Van Dusen, x, xi, xii, xiii, 11, 22, 23, 50, 51, 52-53, 76, 77, 98, 110, 117, 148-149, 156, 157, 158-159, 186, 187, 206, 224, 226, 227, 250, 264-265, 272, 273; Carl Wiens, ix, 294, 295, 296, 297, 298, 299, 300, 301, 302, 303, 304, 305, 306, 307; Terry Workman, 8, 12, 28, 35, 49, 64, 67, 80, 81, 119, 120, 121, 141, 177, 196, 242, 243, 275, 279.